W9-CYD-018

At Issue

Teen Driving

DATE DUE

OCT. 08.2009			
NOV. 05.2009			
NOV. 30.2009			
DEC. 23.2009			
5/3/2010			

HIGHSMITH 45231

Other Books in the At Issue Series:

Are Adoption Policies Fair?

Do Veterans Receive Adequate Health Care?

Foreign Oil Dependence

Guns and Crime

Has No Child Left Behind Been Good for Education?

How Does Advertising Impact Teen Behavior?

How Should the U.S. Proceed in Iraq?

National Security

Reality TV

Senior Citizens and Driving

Should Cameras Be Allowed in Courtrooms?

Should Drilling Be Permitted in the Arctic National
Wildlife Refuge?

Should Governments Negotiate with Terrorists?

Should Juveniles Be Tried as Adults?

Should the Legal Drinking Age Be Lowered?

Should Music Lyrics Be Censored for Violence
and Exploitation?

Should Parents Be Allowed to Choose the Gender of
Their Children?

Should Social Networking Web Sites Be Banned?

What Is the Future of the U.S. Economy?

At Issue

Teen Driving

Louise Gerdes, Book Editor

GREENHAVEN PRESS
A part of Gale, Cengage Learning

Library Media Center
E.O. Smith High School
1235 Storrs Rd.
Storrs, CT 06268

Detroit • New York • San Francisco • New Haven, Conn • Waterville, Maine • London

388.3
Tee

11/08

GALE
CENGAGE Learning

Christine Nasso, *Publisher*
Elizabeth Des Chenes, *Managing Editor*

© 2008 Greenhaven Press, a part of Gale, Cengage Learning.

Gale and Greenhaven Press are registered trademarks used herein under license.

For more information, contact:
Greenhaven Press
27500 Drake Rd.
Farmington Hills, MI 48331-3535
Or you can visit our Internet site at gale.cengage.com

ALL RIGHTS RESERVED.
No part of this work covered by the copyright herein may be reproduced, transmitted, stored, or used in any form or by any means graphic, electronic, or mechanical, including but not limited to photocopying, recording, scanning, digitizing, taping, Web distribution, information networks, or information storage and retrieval systems, except as permitted under Section 107 or 108 of the 1976 United States Copyright Act, without the prior written permission of the publisher.

For product information and technology assistance, contact us at

Gale Customer Support, 1-800-877-4253
For permission to use material from this text or product, submit all requests online at www.cengage.com/permissions

Further permissions questions can be emailed to permissionrequest@cengage.com

Articles in Greenhaven Press anthologies are often edited for length to meet page require-ments. In addition, original titles of these works are changed to clearly present the main thesis and to explicitly indicate the author's opinion. Every effort is made to ensure that Greenhaven Press accurately reflects the original intent of the authors. Every effort has been made to trace the owners of copyrighted material.

Cover photograph reproduced by permission of Images.com/Corbis.

LIBRARY OF CONGRESS CATALOGING-IN-PUBLICATION DATA

Teen driving / Louise Gerdes, book editor.
    p. cm. -- (At issue)
Includes bibliographical references and index.
ISBN 978-0-7377-3940-4 (hbk.)
978-0-7377-3941-1 (pbk.)
    1. Teenage automobile drivers--United States--Juvenile literature. 2. Traffic safety-- United States--Juvenile literature. I. Gerdes, Louise I., 1953-
    HE5620.J8T438 2008
    388.30835'0973--dc22

2008012801

Library Media Center
F.O. Smith High School
1296 Storrs Rd.
Storrs, CT 06268

Printed in the United States of America
1 2 3 4 5 6 7 12 11 10 09 08

Contents

Introduction   **7**

1. An Overview of Teen Driving   **11**
   William Triplett

2. Risk Factors for Teen Drivers Can   **24**
   Prove Fatal
   American Academy of Pediatrics

3. Teen Driving Deaths Are Declining   **32**
   Insurance Institute for Highway Safety

4. Teen Drivers Pose a Dangerous Risk   **35**
   to Others
   AAA Foundation for Traffic Safety

5. Teen Drivers Are No More Dangerous than   **42**
   Adult Drivers
   Mike Males

6. Graduated Licensing Restrictions for Teen   **51**
   Drivers Save Lives
   Melissa A. Savage

7. Current Graduated Licensing Restrictions   **56**
   for Teen Drivers Are Inadequate
   Allan F. Williams

8. Driver Education Does Not Improve   **63**
   Teen Driving Safety
   Allan F. Williams and Susan A. Ferguson

9. Driver Education Lays a Foundation for   **70**
   Safe Teen Driving Skills
   David C. Huff

10. The Driving Age Should Be Increased   **76**
    Robert Davis

11. The Driving Age Should Not Be Increased   **83**
    Allen Robinson

12. Teen Driving Improves When Parents and   **86**
    Teens Agree on Rules
    Kenneth H. Beck, Jessica L. Hartos, and
    Bruce G. Simons-Morton

13. Parents Pass on Bad Driving Habits   **94**
    to Their Teens
    Liberty Mutual and Students Against
    Destructive Decisions

14. Male Teen Passengers Increase Risky   **98**
    Teen Driving
    National Institute of Child Health and
    Human Development

15. Passenger Restrictions for Teen Drivers   **102**
    Will Save Lives
    Anne T. McCartt

16. Teen Cell Phone Use Restrictions Will   **106**
    Save Lives
    Steve Blackistone

Organizations to Contact   **113**

Bibliography   **118**

Index   **122**

Introduction

For most American teens, cars are more than just a form of transportation; cars represent freedom and independence. In the postwar boom of the 1950s, when the economy surged and teens could afford used cars of their own, a new teen car culture was born. American pop culture made driving a car "cool." Indeed, teens see obtaining a driver's license as an important rite of passage. However, cars can also be lethal. When in 1975 the U.S. Department of Transportation began collecting data on automobile accidents, the Fatal Analysis Reporting System (FARS) revealed an alarming trend. More than eighty-seven thousand teens had died on America's roads that year.

During the 1980s, due to the grassroots efforts of organizations such as Mothers Against Drunk Driving (MADD), the public became increasingly alarmed by the problem of teen drunk driving. Research revealed that 41 percent of sixteen- and seventeen-year-olds and 57 percent of eighteen- to twenty-year olds who died in car crashes had a blood alcohol concentration (BAC) of .08 or more. Following the passage of the National Minimum Drinking Age Act (NMDAA) of 1984, which raised the drinking age to twenty-one, the fatality rates dropped significantly to 27 and 44 percent, respectively. During the 1980s and 1990s, some states added laws that suspended the licenses of teens caught driving under the influence of alcohol. In 2000 the federal government required states seeking transportation funds to reduce from 1.0 to .08 the BAC level that determines when a driver of any age is legally driving drunk. Some claim that these changes also contributed to subsequent reductions in teen driving fatalities.

The number of teen drivers killed each year, however, remains disproportionately high. In fact, car crashes are the leading cause of death for American teenagers. Not until the 1990s, however, did states begin to address the fact that teen driving itself seemed to pose a significant risk for teen drivers and their passengers. According to Allan Williams of the Insurance Institute for Highway Safety, "I've studied this problem for 25 years, and for a long time nobody paid attention to it at all." While the concept of reducing teen driving deaths through graduated driver's licenses (GDLs) goes back to the 1970s, "it wasn't until the mid-1990s that it got started," Williams claims, "and I don't know why. It's always been kind of a mystery."

Many believe that more should be done to reduce the risks of teen driving. Because state laws vary so widely, however, researchers find it difficult to get an accurate picture of what policies will best address the problem. For example, Florida and North Carolina reported a 9 and 27 percent reduction in fatal teen crashes, respectively, following the first year each state implemented a GDL program. Because Florida's and North Carolina's GDL laws differ, the reasons why North Carolina's law led to a greater reduction in teen traffic fatalities than Florida's law remains unclear. Analysts not only disagree over which policies are best but also who should hold the primary responsibility for developing and enforcing these policies. The debate over whether this responsibility should remain with the states or shift to parents or even the federal government is reflective of the overarching controversies surrounding the teen driving issue.

Some commentators contend that states should remain primarily responsible for enacting policies to reduce the risks of teen driving. Many argue, however, that to reduce teen driving deaths, state GDL programs must be stronger. All states, these analysts assert, should add passenger restrictions and later curfews to their GDL programs. In fact, 87 percent of teens who died in crashes in 2002 were passengers of teen drivers, and 41 percent of teen driving deaths occurred between 9:00 PM and 6:00 AM. Advocates for Highway and Auto Safety, MADD, the National Transportation Safety Board, the

National Safety Council, and AAA (American Automobile Association) have all asked state legislatures to pass such laws. Critics of increased teen driving restrictions claim that such laws are difficult for the police to enforce and are therefore inadequate to reduce the risks of teen driving. Even Williams, who generally favors stronger GDL programs, observes, "GDL laws are sometimes so complex that police don't even know what they are."

Since it is often difficult for the police to enforce GDL laws, some advocates claim that parents should be the enforcers of passenger restrictions and curfews. In fact, most advocacy groups encourage parents to be more involved. According to Eileen Buckholtz of teendriving.com, "parents [should] log 100 hours minimum driving with their kids, taking them out in bad conditions, showing them the situations they may encounter and giving them a chance to practice." Some states do require that parents be part of the student driving process, but whether parents actually fulfill the requirement is unclear. "We have to go on the parents' word," claims Jeff Tosi of the Maryland Motor Vehicle Administration. Indeed, some argue that parents may not be the best role models. A Students Against Destructive Decisions (SADD) and Liberty Mutual Insurance survey revealed that parents are the greatest influence on teen drivers. Unfortunately, the survey also revealed that parents often engage in risky driving behaviors such as talking on cell phones, driving without seat belts, and speeding.

Some analysts suggest that the federal government link federal highway funds to state compliance with national GDL standards. Since federal incentives were effective in reducing alcohol-related traffic fatalities, these observers argue that such incentives might also reduce teen driving deaths. Opponents claim that states should not base teen driving restrictions on monetary incentives. According to Adrienne Mandel, a Maryland representative, "I'd rather they base them on wanting to save lives." Other analysts such as Radley Balko of the libertarian Cato Institute and Eric Skrum of the National Motorists Association, a motorists' rights organization, oppose federal interference because, they argue, states are in the best position to determine the policies that work best in their own states.

Whether the states, parents, or the federal government should take action to reduce teen driving fatalities remains controversial. The authors in *At Issue: Teen Driving* join the debate, exploring their views on the nature of teen driving and the policies that will best protect America's youngest drivers.

1

An Overview of Teen Driving

William Triplett

William Triplett writes on issues concerning the arts and sciences in publications such as Smithsonian, Nature, *the* Washington Post, *and* CQ Researcher.

Few dispute that teen drivers are involved in more traffic accidents than any other age group. However, policies to curtail this epidemic generate heated debate. For example, proponents of driver education believe it will improve teen driving safety, while others maintain that driver education puts teen drivers on the road with inadequate driving experience. Some commentators claim that additional driving restrictions such as curfews and limits on the number of underage passengers a teen can drive will reduce teen-driving deaths. Critics contend, however, that such restrictions are hard to enforce. The most controversial proposal regarding teen drivers is to increase the driving age. Brain development experts argue that teens are not biologically mature enough to drive, but parents, weary of ferrying their teens, see teen licensing as a source of relief.

Accidents involving teenagers are disproportionately high throughout the United States. Drivers between ages 15 and 20 make up about only 6.4 percent of the nation's driving population, but for the last 10 years they have been involved in approximately 14 percent of all fatal car crashes.

William Triplett, "Teen Driving," *CQ Researcher*, vol. 15, January 7, 2005. Copyright © 2005 by CQ Press, published by CQ Press, a division of Congressional Quarterly Inc. All rights reserved. Reproduced by permission.

An Epidemic

In 2003, nearly 7,900 teen drivers were involved in fatal accidents in the United States. Nearly half of them died, but most of the victims were passengers, drivers or passengers of other vehicles, or pedestrians. Another 308,000 teen drivers were injured in fatal crashes. About 6,000 teens died in automobile accidents in 2003, including 3,657 young drivers.

"Traffic crashes are the leading cause of death" for teens of driving age.

Although those figures were down from the year before—when 3,838 teen drivers were killed—the trend over the last decade has been upward. Since 1993, deaths of drivers 15–20 years old have increased 13 percent. Indeed, says Kristen Kreibich-Staruch, manager of safety programs and communications at DaimlerChrysler Corp., "traffic crashes are the leading cause of death" for teens of driving age. According to the Insurance Institute for Highway Safety (IIHS), motor vehicle crashes account for about 40 percent of adolescent fatalities.

Moreover, teenage drivers are involved in more crashes—fatal and non-fatal—than any other age group. The Centers for Disease Control and Prevention (CDC) reports that in 2002 the motor vehicle death rate for teens (drivers as well as passengers) between ages 15 and 19 was 27.6 deaths per 100,000 population compared to 17.8 for people between 25 and 34 and 15.8 for those between 35 and 44.

Jeffrey W. Runge, a physician who heads the National Highway Transportation Safety Administration (NHTSA), has described teen driving deaths in the United States as "an epidemic.". . .

Looking for Answers

Some experts say that just because teens are allowed to drive at 16 (or even younger) does not necessarily mean they have the maturity to handle the physical or psychological challenges of driving, especially when egged on by their friends. For instance, a 16-year-old girl described as a model student and daughter died in a crash while playing "road-hog" with a friend in another car.

Inexperience is another factor: New drivers simply aren't aware of the many unexpected conditions they might confront, and they know even less about how to deal with them.

"They're always either understeering or oversteering, going off the road or hitting the curb, or turning too soon or too late," says Virginia driving school owner Larry Blake. "I've fought in two wars, and I can tell you, this is the most dangerous profession there is."

As Allan F. Williams, chief scientist for the IIHS, has put it, "You've got several things going on here—a risky driving style; inability to recognize or respond to dangerous driving situations and overconfidence in their abilities. When you put all those things together, you've got a pretty lethal combination."

Graduated Driver Licensing

Some 45 states and the District of Columbia have responded to the problem by instituting graduated driver licensing (GDL) programs, which limit a new driver's privileges pending successful completion of phases involving increasing levels of risk exposure.

The Journal of Safety Research recently reported that GDL programs have helped reduce teen crash rates, but because of differences in state program and evaluation methods, precise nationwide measures cannot be made. And states don't enforce all parts of their GDL programs equally, making them less effective than they could be, advocates say.

But one factor clearly appears to help: raising the legal driving age. In England, where drivers must be age 17, and in Germany, where the age is 18, teens have lower fatality rates than in the United States.

Some experts say more educational programs are needed; others contend they have little impact on teens. And still others argue for more parental involvement in teens' driving lessons. But a recent study by Liberty Mutual Insurance Co. and Students Against Destructive Decisions (SADD) indicated that more parental involvement actually can have a negative effect.

Meanwhile, an upcoming explosion in the number of teenagers is putting new pressure on safety experts to improve teen driving. Reflecting a nationwide trend, the California Office of Traffic Safety recently released a study forecasting a one-third rise in the state's teen population by 2007. The increase will occur because the teenage children of Baby Boomers—who delayed having children to pursue careers—are reaching puberty.

"Teenage traffic deaths could sky-rocket over the next decade," California officials said.

As parents, school officials and safety experts seek ways to better protect teen drivers, here are some of the key questions under debate:

Some experts say formal evaluations of high school "driver ed" programs show they have little or no effect in reducing crashes.

Is Driver Education Effective?

For many teens and parents, the value of driver education—behind-the-wheel experience bolstered by classroom instruction—seems self-evident.

However, some experts say formal evaluations of high school "driver ed" programs show they have little or no effect in reducing crashes.

"Driver education programs are usually short-term, and only basic skills are learned," says Williams, of the IIHS.

"There's not enough time to do more. To think this short-term course is going to make young people safe drivers is kind of unrealistic."

Having studied teen crash rates for 25 years, Williams concluded in a 2004 report: "There is no difference in the crash records of driver education graduates compared with equivalent groups of beginners who learned to drive without formal education."

NHTSA Administrator Runge essentially concurs. "As it's currently configured, driver's education might make a difference in the first six months of driving," he said, "but after that, it doesn't matter much."

Eric Skrum, communications director for the National Motorists Association (NMA), argues that current driver education programs don't put enough emphasis on behind-the-wheel experience. "Instead of telling kids about a skid, you need to get them into a skid," Skrum says. "Teach them how to handle the situation. The few hours that new drivers have now isn't training them for all situations they're going to be in."

While critics acknowledge that high school programs can teach good driving skills, they say the programs have little or no effect on teen attitudes. Indeed, the IIHS maintains that teenagers who have accidents are the least susceptible to behavior change through education.

Studies involving mostly young males have noted the "interrelationship among certain personality traits (rebelliousness, risk-taking, independence, defiance of authority), deviant driving practices (speeding, driving while impaired) and crashes and violations," the IIHS says. "The traits, values and peer associations of this high-risk group are such that changing their behavior through education is a difficult task."

That is the very point that critics fail to understand, according to certified driving instructor Syed Ahmad, of Alexandria, Va. "When accidents happen, they always blame the driver's-ed classes," Ahmad says. "But the fact is, if your intention is to go out and party when you get your license, you're not going to make it."

The DeKalb Study

Allen Robinson, chief executive officer of the American Driver and Traffic Safety Education Association (ADTSEA), says critics of driver education rely heavily—and inappropriately—on a 1974 study in DeKalb County (Macon), Ga. "When we planned the DeKalb study, we were too ambitious," he says. "We said we could reduce fatalities of 16-year-old drivers by 10 percent [through driver's education]. But we only achieved about a 4 percent reduction. So, it was unsuccessful in that respect. But today there isn't a single countermeasure—seat belts or anything—that can show a 4 percent reduction in fatalities."

Yet critics continue to cite the DeKalb study, Robinson asserts, "as the benchmark for why driver's education 'doesn't work.'" Indeed, the study is one of the reasons many high schools discontinue their driver education courses.

If more schools enforced standards more rigorously, . . . driver ed would be highly effective.

However, Robinson says the Oregon Department of Transportation (ODOT) and the Center for Applied Research recently found "significantly lower rates of convictions, suspensions and crashes" for drivers who took a driver ed course versus drivers who learned through 50 hours of informal, supervised driving. An ODOT spokesperson says the report is still in draft form and under review, with no public release date set.

Inconsistent Driver Ed Standards

Driving school owner Blake (who says his pupils have included the daughters of former Presidents Richard Nixon and

Gerald Ford), argues that not all schools evaluate students properly. In Virginia, he notes, instructors can waive a student's school road test if they feel the student has performed well during the course. Increasingly, though, commercial instructors are waiving their road tests for financial reasons, he says.

"When students find out an instructor is going to make them take the road test, they tell their friends, and those friends make sure they don't go to that driving school," Blake says. "More and more schools are waiving the road test because they're scared of losing business." If more schools enforced standards more rigorously, he claims, driver ed would be highly effective.

Indeed, some observers blame the lack of uniformity among driver ed curricula, not driver education per se. "It's all very uneven around the country," says Eileen Buckholtz, the mother of two young drivers and the administrator of the Web site teendriving.com, which advocates safe driving.

Stephen Wallace, chairman and chief executive officer of Students Against Destructive Decisions (SADD), adds, "There's a range of driver education programs out there, so a differing degree of effectiveness exists."

At a 2003 National Transportation Safety Board (NTSB) symposium on driver education, several safety experts argued for uniform, national standards for driver education. But Barbara Harsha, executive director of the Governors Highway Safety Association (GHSA), thinks that would be a mistake. "The states get no federal money for driver's education, so there's no way to make them comply with [national] standards." She favors encouraging states to adopt voluntary core requirements and guidelines for driver ed courses.

"Federal driver education standards would be a terrible idea," agrees Radley Balko, a policy analyst at the Cato Institute, a libertarian think tank. "Every state's driving is a little different—the skills you need to drive in Florida and in

Alaska are quite different. States know better what's best for learning how to drive on their highways."

Yet, no one even knows how many states still offer driver's education in public high schools. "We know that about 55 percent of public high schools in the United States still offer it," Robinson of ADTSEA says, "but we don't know how many states."

Graduated driver licensing (GDL) programs ... are the most popular and widely used method of limiting teen driving.

Limits Imposed on Teen Drivers

Graduated driver licensing (GDL) programs—used in some 45 states and the District of Columbia—are the most popular and widely used method of limiting teen driving. GDL programs generally feature three phases: a learner's permit, which allows driving only when supervised by a fully licensed adult; a provisional, or intermediate, license, which allows unsupervised driving under restricted circumstances and, finally, full licensure. The ages for each phase are usually 15, 16 and 17, respectively.

The first two phases require minimum training periods—varying from state to state—before the student can advance.

The theory behind GDL is simple. "By restricting when teenagers may drive, and with whom, graduated driver licensing allows new drivers to gain much-needed, on-the-road experience in controlled, lower-risk settings," according to NHTSA. "It also means that a teenager will be a little older and more mature when he or she gains a full, unrestricted license."

New Zealand first introduced GDL in 1987, and three subsequent studies of the program, showed positive effects. In 1996, Florida became the first state to initiate a GDL program, and a susequent evaluation showed that it substantially reduced teen deaths. So did later evaluations of GDL programs in California, Connecticut, Kentucky, Michigan, North Carolina, Ohio, Maryland and Oregon. Ohio, for example, reported that following its 1999 implementation of GDL laws, fatal crashes involving 16- and 17-year-old drivers dropped by 70 percent.

While the collective fatality rates of 15-to-20-year-old drivers and passengers have been rising, statistics for specific ages support the effectiveness of GDL programs. For instance, the overwhelming majority of drivers in GDL programs are either 15 or 16. According to the CDC's National Center for Health Statistics, 491 15-year-olds died in motor vehicle accidents in 2000, but the death toll dropped to 422 in 2001. Motor vehicle deaths of 16-year-olds during the same period decreased from 933 to 908.

But the next year, 2002, deaths in both age groups began creeping back up—to 479 for 15-year-olds and 1,046 for 16-year-olds.

Nightime Driving

Harsha of the GHSA suggests the increase was due to lax enforcement. Not all states enforce GDL laws equally, and some of the laws are weak. Harsha's group would like more states with GDL laws to limit nighttime driving and the number of passengers allowed in the vehicle with the teenage driver. "Research shows benefits of these things when they're enforced," she says.

Driving at night is generally more hazardous for all age groups. But for teens it can be especially dangerous. According to the *Journal of Safety Research*, many newly licensed drivers have had less practice driving at night than during the day. "Fatigue—thought to be a problem for teenagers at all times of the day—may be more of a factor at night; and recreational driving that is considered to be high risk, sometimes involving alcohol use, is more likely to take place at night."

For 16-year-old drivers, the risk of a fatal crash is three times higher after 9 PM than during the daytime. Overall, about 40 percent of teen motor vehicle fatalities occur at night.

But most state GDL programs only impose a curfew on teen drivers after midnight or 1 AM. In any case, teen curfews are hard to enforce at any hour, according to Harsha, because police have little way of knowing whether a young person driving at night is underage.

The Risk of Carrying Passengers

The presence of teenage passengers also strongly increases crash risk for teenage drivers. Four studies have confirmed that the risk of an accident increases as more passengers ride with a teenage driver. One study demonstrated that just a single passenger nearly doubled the risk of a fatal crash, and two or more passengers raised the risk to five times that of driving alone. Yet 29 states do not limit the number of passengers that can ride with teen drivers.

Surprisingly, parents often oppose impeding more limits on teen passengers. For instance, Maryland state Del. [delegate] Adrienne A. Mandel has tried for three years to enact legislation that would prohibit teenagers with provisional licenses from carrying any passengers under age 18 except family members. Her attempts have failed each time, she says, mostly because rural families oppose the measure.

"They say more young people will be on the roads if each one has to drive alone," Mandel says. But car-pooling could alleviate that, she points out. Parents in rural areas also complain that passenger limitations would be especially inconvenient in those areas where transportation options aren't abundant, Mandel says. "They're talking about inconvenience. I'm talking about saving lives," she says. Parents also opposed earlier curfews for teens because older teens often have jobs and need a way to get to work at night, she points out.

Teens themselves are often divided over limitations on driving, including GDL programs in general. In 1998, when Delaware was considering adopting a GDL system, a teenager unhappy with the idea wrote to the Website teenink.com: "Getting a driver's license means freedom, and most of us can give you the number of years, months and days until that wonderful moment. You get to say good-bye to the yellow school bus, meet your friends or go to work."

Yet, in early 2004 when South Dakota pushed back its curfew for teen drivers from 8 PM to 10 PM, a 16-year-old girl who welcomed the later curfew still admitted that, "when I first started driving, it really scared me being out in the dark."

The IIHS advocates earlier curfews and uniform restrictions on teen passengers, and the NTSB says teens should not be allowed to use cell phones while driving.

"Young and inexperienced drivers out late at night with limited practice and with other kids in the car—there are limits for those drivers that clearly make sense," says Wallace of SADD. "But to some degree, this comes down to education and practice. At some point, they're all inexperienced—they have to get out there and learn."

"And when they start, those are the ones we have to look out for, because nearly one in five 16-year-old drivers is involved in an accident in their first year."

Should the Driving Age Be Raised?

Teen drivers between the ages of 16 and 19 have the highest fatal and non-fatal crash rates in the country, but 16-year-olds are three times more likely to be involved in a crash than 19-year-olds. Every decade, more than 9,000 16-year-olds die in motor vehicle accidents in the United States.

Many safety experts blame the fact that states—including those with graduated driver licensing—grant unsupervised driving privileges at 16, which many safety advocates argue is too soon.

Besides being emotionally and psychologically immature, young, new drivers face other challenges when making decisions and judgments. Susan Scharoun, chairman of the psychology department at Le Moyne College, in Syracuse, N.Y., notes that biological factors influence teenage behavior, particularly when risk-taking is involved. Recent research shows that hormonal activity and incomplete development of the frontal lobe of the brain, which controls reasoning and memory, affect teen risk-taking behavior, according to Scharoun.

Thus, 16-year-olds' emotional, psychological and biological immaturity—combined with their inexperience—explain why they have the highest percentages of single-vehicle crashes and crashes involving speeding and driver error, as well as the highest vehicle-occupancy rates, according to the IIHS.

High crash rates of U.S. teenagers lead many ... to recommend that states raise their minimum driving ages.

American teenagers are allowed to drive at younger ages than in most other countries. In Northern Europe, for instance, the minimum age for a beginning driver is typically 18; in England, it's 17. By contrast, an adolescent in Michigan can obtain a learner's permit at 14 years and nine months.

But the high crash rates of U.S. teenagers lead many—like Syracuse, N.Y., high school driver education instructor Ed Bregande—to recommend that states raise their minimum driving ages. He thinks learner's permits should not be issued to anyone younger than 17.

"You hear talk of raising the age now and then," says Williams of the IIHS. "But the political reality is that whenever it has come up, it never goes anywhere."

"I think 16 certainly is too young to drive," concurs Harsha of the Governors Highway Safety Association. "But it's very difficult politically, especially in farm states, to raise the age. There's not enough public or political support yet for increasing the age. Possibly in the future."

Parents are often the biggest obstacle to raising the driving age.

Obstacles to Raising the Driving Age

Parents are often the biggest obstacle to raising the driving age. As one mother has put it, "When they get their license and they can drive themselves to practice and then drive home, for me, it was great."

Williams explains that parents face a dilemma: They want their kids to start driving as soon as possible so the parents don't have to chauffeur them around anymore. "But they also know it's dangerous for kids to drive," he says.

Teens are predictable on the issue. Asked if the minimum driving age should be raised to help reduce teen accident and fatality rates, a 16-year-old student at Northern Virginia Driving School answers for the entire class when he says, "Sure, right after they give me my license."

2

Risk Factors for Teen Drivers Can Prove Fatal

American Academy of Pediatrics

The American Academy of Pediatrics is an organization of pediatricians committed to the physical, mental, and social health and well-being of infants, children, adolescents, and young adults.

Teen drivers share characteristics that increase their chances of being involved in an automobile accident, the leading cause of death for teens. Not only do teen drivers lack experience, they also overestimate their driving skills. In addition, teen drivers take greater chances, especially in the face of peer pressure. Indeed, the likelihood of their being involved in a car crash is proportional to the number of passengers teen drivers carry. The risks to their safety increase even further when teens drive at night, especially if they have been drinking. Moreover, teen drivers are less likely to wear seat belts and often drive smaller, older cars.

Motor vehicle crashes continue to be the leading cause of death for 16- to 20-year-olds, accounting for approximately 5500 occupant fatalities annually (27 deaths per 10,000 population). Each year, approximately 450,000 teenagers are injured, and 27,000 of them require hospitalization. Of those killed, approximately 63% are drivers and 37% are passengers. Two thirds of the teenagers who die in automobile crashes are male.

American Academy of Pediatrics, "The Teen Driver," *Pediatrics*, vol. 118, December 2006, pp. 2570–2720. Copyright © 2006 American Academy of Pediatrics. Used with permission.

In 2004, 7700 teenaged drivers were involved in a crash in which someone died. Although the 12 million adolescent drivers represent only approximately 6% of total drivers, they account for approximately 14% of the fatal crashes. In terms of total crashes per million miles driven, 16- to 19-year-olds have a crash rate almost twice that of 20- to 24-year-olds, almost 3 times that of 25- to 29-year-olds, and more than 4 times that of 30- to 69-year olds. Within the 16- to 19-year age range, the youngest drivers have the highest risk. The crash rate for 16-year-olds (35 crashes per million miles) is much higher than that even for 17-year-olds (20 crashes per million miles) and is almost 9 times greater than that of the general population of drivers (4 crashes per million miles).

Motor vehicle crashes continue to be the leading cause of death for 16- to 20-year-olds.

Inexperience

The adolescent, as a novice driver, lacks the experience and ability to perform many of the complex tasks of ordinary driving. Compared with experienced drivers, the novice adolescent driver is less proficient in detecting and responding to hazards and controlling the vehicle, especially at higher speeds. The risk of having a crash during the learner-permit stage is low, because the teenager is supervised and is generally not driving in high-risk conditions. In contrast, data from Nova Scotia show that the highest crash rate is seen during the first month after the teenager gets his or her license (120 crashes per 10,000 drivers). After the first month, the crash rate decreases rather quickly over the next 5 months (70 crashes per 10,000 drivers) and then shows a slower decline for the next 18 months (50 crashes per 10,000 drivers). Because rapid improvement is seen over such a short time period, inexperience appears to be a much more important factor in crash rates than young age. Although these data also show that driver experience improves driving skills, traditional driver education programs usually provide only 6 hours of on-the-road training.

In 2004, 38% of male and 25% of female drivers 15 to 20 years of age involved in fatal crashes were speeding at the time of the crash.

Risk Taking

It is normal for adolescents to take chances, succumb to peer pressures, overestimate their abilities, and have emotional mood swings. These behaviors can all place the teenaged driver at greater risk of having automobile crashes. Males seem to be at especially high risk, possibly as a result of social norms and media images that equate fast driving and ability to perform difficult driving maneuvers as masculine. In 2004, 38% of male and 25% of female drivers 15 to 20 years of age involved in fatal crashes were speeding at the time of the crash. These rates were higher than for any other age group. It must be stressed, however, that the great majority of nonfatal crashes involving 16-year-old drivers result from inexperience rather than from speeding or patently risky behavior.

There is evidence from MRI [magnetic resonance imaging] research that the prefrontal cortex (the area of the brain responsible for planning, impulse control, and executive decision-making) does not mature fully until the early to mid-20s. Although some legislators are using such brain-development research to support limits on teenaged driving, no scientific data have yet been published that link driving behavior to neuroimaging findings.

Teenaged Passengers

With adolescent drivers, the chance of being involved in a car crash is directly proportional to the number of teenager passengers being transported. Compared with driving alone, 16- to 17-year-olds have a 40% increased risk of crashing when they have 1 friend in the car, double the risk with 2 passengers, and almost 4 times the risk with 3 or more teenaged passengers. This relationship was not seen with adult drivers and is much less marked with 18- to 19-year-old drivers.

The most dangerous way a teenager can get to and from school is by driving in a car with a teenaged driver. Open-campus school lunch policies, in which groups of teenagers drive away from school to eat, are also associated with high crash rates. The underlying reasons that teenaged passengers increase driving risk are not clear. In addition to general distraction, intentional encouragement of risky driving behavior and other social interactions may play a role. For both male and female teenaged drivers, the presence of a male passenger results in faster speeds and more risky driving behaviors than does the presence of a female passenger.

For young teenaged drivers, fatal nighttime crashes are more likely to be associated with multiple teenaged passengers, speeding, and alcohol use.

Nighttime Driving

Young teenaged drivers (16- and 17-year-olds) have a higher rate of nighttime crashes than do drivers of any other age group. Before nighttime driving curfews were instituted widely, only 14% of the miles driven by 16- to 17-year-old drivers occurred between 9 PM and 6 AM, yet this time period accounted for 32% of fatal crashes in this age group. Although nighttime restrictions for teenagers commonly limit driving after midnight, 58% of the fatal nighttime crashes occur in the 3-hour period before midnight. For young teenaged drivers, fatal nighttime crashes are more likely to be associated with multiple teenaged passengers, speeding, and alcohol use. Although it is inherently more difficult to drive in the dark for drivers of all ages, fatigue and lack of practice may play a greater role for teenagers.

Alcohol, Marijuana, and Medications

During the period 1982–2001, fatal alcohol-related crash rates decreased by 60% for 16- to 17-year-old drivers. In 1982, 31% of teenagers fatally injured had an especially high blood alcohol concentration (BAC) of 0.10% or greater, but this statistic dropped to 12% by 1995–2001. Teenagers drink and drive less often than adults, but their crash risks are higher than adults when they do drink, especially at low and moderate BACs. In the 2005 Youth Risk Behavior Surveillance Study, 9.9% of 9th-through 12th-graders said that in the last month they had driven after drinking, and 28.5% admitted to riding with a driver who had been drinking.

The prevalence of acute marijuana use among drivers is estimated to be 1% to 6%. Of those drivers involved in severe injury crashes, positive cannabis levels or self-reports of recent use have been found in higher numbers (6%–25%), suggesting a relationship between marijuana and crashes. Much, but not all, of this relationship may be the result of other risky driving habits (positive BAC, no seat belt, speeding, sleepy while driving) that often are associated with marijuana use.

In a study of 414 injured drivers (all ages) in Colorado, urine toxicology assays detected marijuana more frequently than alcohol (17% vs 14%). Evidence from experimental studies has demonstrated impaired performance on various driving skills tests after the use of marijuana. Furthermore, when just moderate doses of alcohol and marijuana were used together, a dramatic deterioration in driving performance (swerving, slowed reaction time) resulted.

A variety of prescription and over-the-counter medications, such as sedatives, analgesics, sedating antihistamines, stimulants, and antihypertensives, may have detrimental effects on driving abilities. Drug combinations and drugs mixed with alcohol can be especially problematic. A single 50-mg dose of diphenhydramine has been shown to have a greater effect on driving performance than a BAC of 0.10%. Failure to warn patients about the possibility of driving impairment from medications has resulted in successful lawsuits against physicians.

Safety Belts

As with adults, low safety belt use by teenagers results in preventable injuries and deaths. Approximately 82% of all motorists wear safety belts, but the rate reported by the National Center for Statistics and Analysis for 16- to 24-year-olds is 77%. In a study of teenaged drivers who were observed arriving at high school, only 62% were wearing their seat belts. The passengers of these teenaged drivers wore restraints only 47% of the time. Analysis of fatal crashes with teenage drivers demonstrates that safety belt use is lower in high-risk situations (driving under the influence of alcohol, nighttime driving, having multiple teenaged passengers, when the car is older, and when the driver is male or unlicensed or has a suspended license). Safety belts were used by only 18% of drivers with a BAC of 0.10% or higher, compared with 40% of sober drivers.

For teenaged occupants, approximately 58% of those who were killed in automobile crashes in 2004 were unbelted.

For teenaged occupants, approximately 58% of those who were killed in automobile crashes in 2004 were unbelted. Because safety belts have been shown to be 45% effective in preventing front-seat fatalities, many of these deaths could have been prevented. Air bags alone have been found to be only 10% effective in preventing deaths. The reasons teenagers give for not wearing seat belts include not "cool," peer pressure, wrinkles clothes, traveling short distance, and feeling that "nothing will happen to me." Almost half of teenagers (47%) say they feel that safety belts are "as likely to cause harm as to help," 27% said wearing a safety belt makes them "worry more about being in an accident," and 30% indicated they would feel "self-conscious if they were going against the group norm in wearing safety belts." Only 27% of the actors playing motor vehicle occupants in 25 recent G-rated and PG-rated films were portrayed wearing safety belts.

Driving Unsafe Cars

There is evidence that adolescents are more likely than adults to drive smaller and older-model cars, especially if the teen is the owner of the car. This is problematic, because smaller cars provide less crash protection than larger cars, and older-model cars often have fewer modern safety features. When teenagers drive sport utility vehicles, they are significantly more likely to have a rollover than are drivers older than 24 years. Sporty cars with high-performance features may encourage speeding. One survey showed that parents choose cars for their teenagers more on the basis of price and style than on the basis of safety features.

Distractions in the Car

Distractions are contributing factors for motor vehicle crashes for both adolescents and adults. Eating, drinking, and adjusting the radio or the climate controls each cause more crashes than cellular phone use. Cellular phone use has been estimated to increase crash rates by fourfold, and hands-free models are not associated with significantly less risk. There is some evidence that distractions may be a greater problem for the inexperienced driver. Distracted novice drivers tend to glance away from the road for longer periods of time, during which they have trouble responding to hazards and staying in their lane.

Unlicensed Drivers

Drivers without valid licenses (unlicensed, revoked, suspended) tend to be younger and male, are more apt to have been involved in a fatal nighttime crash or to have a recent conviction for driving while intoxicated, and are more likely to have had multiple license suspensions. Approximately 5% of drivers younger than 20 years who have been involved in a fatal crash were driving with their license suspended or revoked, and 10% had never held a license. Unlicensed teenaged drivers are 5 times more likely to have had a conviction for driving while intoxicated and 3 times more likely to have had a previous license suspension than are fatally injured teenagers with valid licenses.

Attention-Deficit/Hyperactivity Disorder

Teenaged drivers with attention-deficit/hyperactivity disorder (ADHD) are 2 to 4 times more likely to be injured in a motor vehicle crash than are their peers without ADHD. They are also more likely to have repeat traffic citations and to have their licenses suspended or revoked. Driving performance of teenagers with ADHD seems to improve with psychostimulant medication, primarily because of decreased errors of inattentiveness. Compared with 3-times-a-day dosing of methylphenidate, longer-acting, controlled-release medication may result in better driving throughout the day and, particularly, during the evening hours.

3

Teen Driving Deaths Are Declining

Insurance Institute for Highway Safety

The Insurance Institute for Highway Safety is a research and educational organization dedicated to reducing deaths, injuries, and property damage related to vehicle crashes on America's highways.

Teen driving deaths have been on the decline. Indeed, statistics show that in 2005, teen driving fatalities were at their lowest since 1992. Between 1996 and 2005, for example, the number of fatal crashes fell 41 percent among teens carrying passengers, but the greatest reduction in fatalities was among nighttime teen drivers, which fell by 48 percent. Reductions in teen driving fatalities coincide with an increase in state graduated licensing laws that delay the driving age, restrict nighttime driving, and limit the number of teen passengers.

There's a lot to cheer about when it comes to teenage drivers, especially 16 year-olds. Although their crash rates remain higher than those of adults, real progress has been made in safeguarding these young beginning drivers.

Graduated Licensing Laws

Two years ago [in 2005] the Institute reported a sharp drop in the fatal crash rate for 16-year-old drivers after states began

Insurance Institute for Highway Safety, "Good News About Teen Drivers," *Status Report*, vol. 42, June 15, 2007, pp. 1–2, 6. Copyright © 1996–2006, Insurance Institute for Highway Safety, Highway Loss Data Institute. Reproduced by permission.

enacting graduated licensing laws in the 1990's. Fatal crash involvement based on the population of 16 year-olds fell 26 percent during 1993–2003.

A new study from the Institute shows continued progress in reducing fatal and nonfatal crashes per population of 16-year-old drivers, and these gains haven't been offset by higher crash rates among older teenagers. Between 1996 and 2005 both fatal and police-reported crashes per population fell about 40 percent for 16 year-olds, about 25 percent for 17 year-olds, and about 15–19 percent for 18 year-olds.

Teenage drivers long have been considered to pose the greatest risk to themselves and other road users, and for good reason. Based on crashes of all severities, the crash rate per mile driven for 16–19 year-olds is 4 times the rate for drivers 20 and older. Risk is highest at age 16.

Nighttime fatal crashes . . . among 16-year-old drivers decreased 48 percent during 1996–2005. This compares with a 40 percent decline in daytime fatal crashes.

Graduated Licensing Leads to Fewer Fatalities

A closer look at the statistics shows that the picture is improving. The number of teens killed in crashes in 2005 was the lowest since 1992, despite the largest teen population since 1977. During 2005, 3,889 passenger vehicle occupants ages 16–19 were killed on US roads, and an estimated 1.9 million were involved in police-reported crashes. This was 8 percent fewer deaths and 20 percent fewer police-reported crashes than occurred in 1996 for this age group. Much of the progress has occurred in areas targeted by many graduated licensing laws: fatal nighttime crashes and fatal crashes involving multiple teenage passengers.

Nighttime fatal crashes per population among 16-year-old drivers decreased 48 percent during 1996–2005. This compares with a 40 percent decline in daytime fatal crashes. Non-fatal crashes declined too. Nighttime police-reported crashes fell 47 percent for 16-year-old drivers and 29 percent for 17 year-olds.

One of the most dangerous scenarios is when a teen driver ferries other teens. This kind of fatal crash fell 41 percent between 1996 and 2005. At the same time, fatal crashes involving 16 year-olds driving alone fell 24 percent. The proportion of fatally injured drivers with positive blood alcohol concentrations fell by 16 percent for 16 year-olds and 5–9 percent for 17–19 year-olds from 1996 to 2005.

"We didn't set out to evaluate the effectiveness of graduated licensing laws, but our findings are consistent with the increased presence of such laws, many of which restrict nighttime driving and driving with teenage passengers in the vehicle," says Anne McCartt, Institute senior vice president for research and one of the authors of the study. Graduated driver licensing delays full licensure while allowing beginners to get their initial driving experience under lower risk conditions. Since 1995, all states have implemented some elements of graduated licensing.

"We can't definitively point to graduated licensing or other factors that would explain the big drop in fatal crashes among teenagers," McCartt says. "It may be because teens were licensed for less time during the year they turned 16 or because restrictions on when and with whom they could drive reduced their exposure. It also could be that the beginners in this study drove more safely because of longer learner's permit periods. Some or all of these factors may have contributed to the decline."

4

Teen Drivers Pose a Dangerous Risk to Others

AAA Foundation for Traffic Safety

The AAA (American Automobile Association) Foundation for Traffic Safety funds research projects designed to discover the causes of traffic crashes, prevent them, and minimize injuries.

The majority of those killed in fatal teen driving accidents are not teen drivers but passengers, the occupants of other vehicles, and nonmotorists. Indeed, automobile crashes involving a fifteen-, sixteen-, or seventeen-year-old driver led to the death of 30,917 people between 1995 and 2004. Of those, 31.8 percent were the teen driver's passengers, 24.2 percent were occupants of cars driven by adults, and 7.5 percent were pedestrians, bicyclists, or occupants of nonmoving vehicles. Since the problem of teen driving fatalities is a problem for all drivers, teen driving safety should be a national priority.

The AAA [American Automobile Association] Foundation for Traffic Safety analyzed data from the National Highway Traffic Safety Administration's (NHTSA) Fatality Analysis Reporting System (FARS) from 1995 through 2004, and identified all fatal crashes involving 15-, 16-, and 17-year-old drivers of passenger vehicles.

AAA Foundation for Traffic Safety, "Teen Crashes—Everyone Is at Risk," Washington, DC: AAA Government Relations, 2006. Copyright © 2006 AAA. All rights reserved.

This analysis shows that between 1995 and 2004 crashes involving 15- to 17-year-old drivers claimed the lives of 30,917 people, of which 11,177 (36.2%) were those drivers themselves. However, the majority of fatalities in these crashes were people other than those drivers, and included 9,847 of their passengers, 7,477 occupants of vehicles operated by drivers 18 years of age or older, and 2,323 nonmotorists.

The majority of fatalities in [teen] crashes were people other than [teen] drivers, and included 9,847 of their passengers.

The analysis also shows that while 12,413 of these fatalities occurred in single-vehicle crashes involving only the vehicle operated by the teenage driver, the remaining 18,504 occurred in crashes involving multiple vehicles and/or nonmotorists. Of these, more than half were either occupants of vehicles driven by people at least 18 years of age (7,477, 40.4%) or nonmotorists (2,323, 12.6%). Finally, of the occupants of other vehicles and nonmotorists killed in these crashes, more than four of five were at least 21 years old. . . .

Methods and Definitions

FARS is a census of every motor vehicle crash that involves a motor vehicle in transport, occurs on a roadway in the United States that is customarily open to the public and results in the death of a vehicle occupant or nonmotorist within 30 days. FARS provides information on all crashes meeting these criteria, including all vehicles and people involved. . . .

All crashes involving a 15-, 16-, or 17-year-old driver of a passenger vehicle were identified. Passenger vehicles, as defined by NHTSA, include passenger cars, light trucks, sport utility vehicles and vans. Medium trucks, heavy trucks, buses, tractors, motorcycles, mopeds and other such vehicles are not categorized as passenger vehicles. Crashes involving a 15- to

17-year-old driver of a nonpassenger vehicle do not appear in the analysis reported here unless a 15- to 17-year-old driver of a passenger vehicle was involved in the same crash.

People fatally injured in crashes involving a 15-, 16-, or 17-year-old driver were categorized as:

- 15- to 17-year-old driver

- Passenger of 15- to 17-year-old driver

- Occupant of other vehicle

- Nonmotorist

- Other occupant.

The 15- to 17-year-old driver category includes every fatally injured person ages 15, 16, or 17 who was coded in FARS as a driver of a passenger vehicle. The "passenger of 15- to 17-year-old driver" category includes all people coded in FARS as passenger or unknown occupant type in a motor vehicle in transport, who were coded in FARS as being occupants of a passenger vehicle whose driver was 15, 16, or 17 years old.

The category "occupant of other vehicle" included all occupants (i.e., driver, passenger or unknown occupant type in a motor vehicle in transport) of all types of vehicles in which the driver was coded as being at least 18 years old.

People categorized as "nonmotorist" included pedestrians, bicyclists, occupants of motor vehicles not in transport (e.g., parked), and occupants of nonmotor-vehicle transport devices (e.g., horse-drawn carriages, etc., involved in crashes with a motor vehicle in transport).

Finally, occupants of nonpassenger vehicles (e.g., motorcycles) operated by a 15- to 17-year-old driver, occupants of passenger vehicles driven by people younger than 15 years of age, and occupants of passenger vehicles driven by people of unknown age were classified as "other occupants.". . .

Crashes were classified into three types:

- Single-vehicle

- Single-vehicle and nonmotorist

- Multiple-vehicle

A crash was classified as a single-vehicle crash if it involved only one vehicle (e.g., a passenger vehicle driven by a driver between ages 15 and 17) and no nonmotorists. If a crash involved only the vehicle driven by the 15- to 17-year-old driver, but also involved one or more nonmotorists, it was classified as single-vehicle and nonmotorist. If a crash involved more than one motor vehicle in transport, it was classified as a multiple-vehicle crash. Finally, a parked car is considered a motor vehicle not in transport, and the occupants of a motor vehicle not in transport are considered nonmotorists. Thus, crashes involving one passenger vehicle operated by a 15- to 17-year-old driver and another vehicle that was parked were coded as either single-vehicle or single-vehicle and nonmotorist, depending on whether any nonmotorists were involved in the crash.

Examining the Results

Between 1995 and 2004 26,990 drivers between ages 15 and 17 were involved in 26,453 fatal crashes that claimed the lives of 30,917 people. . . .

Of the 30,917 people who died in crashes involving a 15- to 17-year-old driver 11,177 (36.2%) were the 15- to 17-year-old drivers themselves. Another 9,847 (31.8%) were passengers riding in vehicles driven by 15- to 17-year-old drivers and 7,477 (24.2%) were occupants of vehicles operated by drivers at least 18 years old. Another 2,323 (7.5%) were nonmotorists, which include pedestrians, bicyclists, occupants of motor vehicles not in transport, occupants of nonmotor-vehicle transport devices and other people who were not occupants of motor vehicles in transport. . . .

Of the 18,504 deaths that occurred in [crashes with multiple vehicles or between a single vehicle and nonmotorists], 7,477 (40.4%) were occupants of other vehicles and another 2,323 (12.6%) were nonmotorists (i.e., mostly pedestrians, some bicyclists and very few other types of nonmotorists).

The 15-, 16-, and 17-year-old drivers themselves comprised 4,705 (25.4%) of the multiple-vehicle crash deaths and their passengers accounted for another 3,906 (21.1%). . . .

Another 12,413 (40.0%) deaths occurred in single-vehicle crashes. Of these, 52.1% were the teenage drivers themselves and 47.9% were their passengers. The majority of these single-vehicle crashes involved either rollovers or collisions with trees or utility poles. . . .

Of the 9,847 passengers of 15- to 17-year-old drivers who were killed in crashes, . . . 5,273 (53.5%) were also between ages 15 and 17.

Of the 9,847 passengers of 15- to 17-year-old drivers who were killed in crashes over the period analyzed, 5,273 (53.5%) were also between ages 15 and 17. Another 1,536 (15.6%) were between ages 18 and 20, 1,615 (16.4%) were younger than 15 and 1,401 (14.2%) were 21 or older. . . .

The number of people not riding in vehicles operated by 15- to 17-year-olds, who died in crashes involving 15- to 17-year-old drivers, . . . include occupants of other vehicles, nonmotorists and other occupants, as defined before. 7,969 of these 9,893 people (80.6%) were 21 or older.

Drawing Conclusions

To help reduce teen-driver crashes, AAA set an ambitious goal in 1997 to pass graduated driver licensing, or GDL, laws in all 50 states and the District of Columbia. When Wyoming and Montana approved bills in 2005, that goal was achieved. These legislative efforts have helped save lives by requiring teens to get more practice behind the wheel. However, not all GDL laws are comprehensive, as they lack some important components (e.g., passenger restrictions).

[Teen] crashes also kill pedestrians and people in other vehicles—husbands, mothers, children, brothers and grandmothers.

This analysis shows that the tragedy of teen-driver crashes goes well beyond the teen drivers and their teen passengers. These crashes also kill pedestrians and people in other vehicles—husbands, mothers, children, brothers and grandmothers. That's why . . . AAA is again making teen driver safety the Association's highest priority. AAA clubs across the country will focus on strengthening existing GDL laws, educating parents and creating public/private partnerships to address this problem.

Comprehensive GDL Laws. Since 1997, most states have made improvements to their teen driving laws. However, GDL laws in many states are missing key components. AAA recommends that all GDL laws have three stages with some combination of the following:

- Six- to 12-month learner's permit with at least 50 hours of supervised driving.

- Six- to 12-month intermediate or probationary license with meaningful night and passenger restrictions.

- States should examine their own crash data to determine the starting time for night restrictions. At a minimum, probationary license holders should be restricted from driving from midnight to 5 AM.

- All GDL laws should include meaningful passenger restrictions. At a minimum, teens should be prohibited from transporting other teen passengers for at least six months in the intermediate/probationary license stage. . . .

Parental Involvement. Stronger laws play a part in keeping roads safe for everyone, but parents play a critical role in enforcing these laws and serving as good role models for their children. Since many state laws key provisions, GDL laws should be considered as baselines. Parents in states with weak passenger restrictions should not allow their teen to ride with other teen drivers and should not allow them to transport other teens in the first year of driving. It's tempting to be lured by the convenience of having other options for getting kids to and from school and practices, but the risks are just too great. Recognizing that parents may feel awkward about enforcing rules that other parents are not enforcing, AAA has developed a discussion guide to help parents work as a team to ensure teens gain driving experience in the safest environment possible during that first year. It encourages parents to talk with one another about the driving rules in their respective homes and encourages them to develop some common rules. That way, teens who are friends have the same or similar rules, which helps remove some of the peer pressure to break parental imposed rules, like passenger restrictions, mileage/road limits, etc.

Community Partnerships. Advocacy groups, victims advocates, law enforcement, schools, local businesses, parents and all citizens must band together to address these tragedies. AAA clubs across the country will be bringing together diverse groups to strengthen laws and educate the public about the dangers of teen driving to make the roads safer for everyone.

5

Teen Drivers Are No More Dangerous than Adult Drivers

Mike Males

Mike Males, formerly a professor of sociology at the University of California, Santa Cruz, is currently a senior researcher for the Center on Juvenile and Criminal Justice and the editor of Youth-Facts.org. He is best known for his book Scapegoat Generation, *which dispels many popular myths about youth.*

Commentators who claim that teen drivers are reckless and incapable of making good driving decisions ignore alternative explanations for the greater crash rate among teens. When statistics control for poverty and lack of experience, a comparison reveals little difference in crash rates between teen and adult drivers. In fact, teen crash rates decrease sharply among teens who drive regularly. Thus laws that delay when and under what conditions teens may drive might in fact put all drivers at risk by preventing teen drivers from gaining valuable driving experience.

Reports have depicted teenage drivers as unacceptably dangerous and proposed severe restrictions, or even outright bans, on driving by persons under 18, 21—or even 25, some suggest. A study released in January 2006 by the American Automobile Association's [AAA] Foundation for Traffic Safety, entitled "Teen Crashes: Everyone Is at Risk," stated that drivers ages 15–17 were "involved in . . . fatal crashes that claimed the lives of 30,917 people" from 1995 through 2004. The report accused teen drivers of killing "husbands, mothers, brothers, children, and grandmothers . . . everyone is at risk."

Mike Males, "Teen Drivers: What Are the Real Risks?," *www.youthrights.org*, April 4, 2006. Reproduced by permission. www.youthrights.org/forums/downloads.php?do=file&id=102.

News stories on teen drivers, and companion stories on adolescent brain development, pronounced teens as inherent risk-takers, cognitively incapable of good driving decisions. Experts and reporters variously labeled teens as "reckless," "stupid," "irrational," "crazy," even "alien." In raw numbers, teenaged drivers are involved in more traffic crashes, including fatal ones, per driver and per mile driven than older drivers. Authorities have attributed this discrepancy mainly to adolescents' allegedly innate immaturity, which produces more recklessness and inability to perceive and manage dangerous situations; some also cite lack of driving experience. Nearly all states have implemented restrictions on driving by persons under age 18 or 20, such as graduated drivers' licensing (GDL) laws, which have been reported to reduce teenage traffic accidents, injuries, and fatalities. Even more severe restrictions have been proposed. Persons under 25 shouldn't hold drivers' licenses or vote, Jay Giedd of the National Institute of Mental Health and Laurence Steinberg of Temple University declared. Teens should not be allowed to drive short trips to the store even once, a Washington safety expert said.

Studies on teen driving risks have failed to examine . . . alternative explanations for the greater traffic accident rate among teens and young adults.

Alternative Explanations

Despite the strong, often inflamed commentary, media reports, safety experts, and studies on teen driving risks have failed to examine two crucial factors that provide alternative explanations for the greater traffic accident rate among teens and young adults:

1. *The lower socioeconomic status of adolescents and young adults compared to older adults.* Socioeconomic status—the levels of poverty, income, wealth—are routinely assessed when comparing the behaviors of different population groups such

as races or ethnicities. Yet, researchers have not controlled for socioeconomics when comparing adults and adolescents. In practice, researchers have assumed that teens as a demographic drive under conditions reasonably identical to those of older adults. This is not the case. The percentage of teenagers and young adults living in households with incomes below federal poverty guidelines is two to three times higher than for middle-aged adults. Further, middle-aged adults live in households with incomes twice as high, and total net worths five times higher, compared to those teenagers and young adults occupy. Low-income status has been linked to higher risks of fatality, including traffic fatality. Poorer populations drive older, less safe vehicles, drive on less well-maintained roads, and access lower-quality medical care. If poverty is a factor in traffic crash risk, we would expect to see higher rates of traffic fatalities among both teens and adults per mile driven in poorer areas compared to richer ones.

There is little or no intrinsic difference between teen and adult driving risk; the apparent difference in risks is due to differing conditions, not age.

---

2. *The benefits of teens gaining experience with adult behaviors while young to reduce the risks they later face as adults.* This factor has been acknowledged but largely discounted in the current climate of discussion. Called "learning by doing," this theory holds that it is not teens' immaturity or innate risk-taking, but their lack of practical driving experience, that produces higher rates of traffic fatality. Teenagers who drive more may be more at risk of accidents, but the experience they gain will reduce their accident rates as young adults even more. If this is the case, we would expect to see, (a) teens experiencing lower rates of traffic fatality in areas in which teens drive more miles, and (b) higher rates of traffic fatalities among young adults who, as teens, were restricted from driv-

ing, as by severe GDLs. If this theory is correct, studies that have measured the lives saved by GDLs and other restrictive laws by comparing teenage fatality trends to those of young adults suffer from serious methodological flaws that would strongly exaggerate these laws' effects.

This study's hypothesis, then, is the null one: *There is little or no intrinsic difference between teen and adult driving risk; the apparent difference in risks is due to differing conditions, not age....*

Exaggerated Risk Difference

Even without considering additional factors, the practical risk difference between teenage and adult drivers has been vastly exaggerated. In the 24 California counties studied for 1995–2004, drivers ages 15–19 were involved in 42 fatal crashes per billion miles driven, compared to 15 for drivers aged 45–64. This three-fold higher risk for teen drivers is widely cited as proof that teens and adults think and approach driving in radically different ways.

Teen driving risks ... result from greater poverty and the interrelated factors of driving inexperience, not innate risk-taking.

However, a very different perspective emerges when the fact that serious motor vehicle accidents and fatalities are *very rare events* is considered. In practice, if an average teen and average 45–64 year-old driver each drove from Los Angeles to San Francisco and back 75,000 times (770 miles round trip each, a task which would take a minimum of five lifetimes), the teen would be expected to be involved in crashes causing one additional fatality and three more serious injuries. This is a maximum estimate; the gap between teen and adult drivers ages 20–44, or 65 and older, would be narrower.

The Impact of Poverty and Inexperience

Teen driving risks, overwhelmingly, result from greater poverty and the interrelated factor of driving inexperience, not innate risk-taking. The risks of a teen driver being in a fatal crash are far from uniform; per mile driven, they vary by a staggering 750% from California's richest to poorest counties. When multiple factors are examined, younger age explains only a small fraction of the difference between teen and middle-agers, the safest category of adult drivers. Even though poverty, income, and VMD [vehicle miles driven] are highly inter-correlated, each shows up in the regression as a separate, strong predictor of motor vehicle fatality risk for all ages....

The Impact of Experience and Driving Conditions

Where teens drive a lot, they quickly improve—so much so that teens who drive a lot are actually safer on an absolute basis than teens who drive very little. Higher-income teens are safer than low-income teens not just due to their access to safer vehicles, driving conditions, medical care, and other benefits, but because *they drive many more miles per day.* In fact, despite driving more miles, teens in several more affluent counties are at lower *absolute* risk of deadly crashes than both teens and adult drivers of all ages in the poorest counties. Driving conditions and experience, not age, best predict fatal crash propensities.

Under equal conditions, teens are no riskier than drivers over age 65.

Where teen and adult drivers experience similar conditions, their driving risks are similar as well. When compared straight across, the risk of teen drivers' involvement in fatal traffic crashes is nearly three times higher than for middle-aged drivers. However, when poverty rates are equalized, a different picture emerges. In California's 24 largest counties, the poverty rate among California's older teenagers ranges from 8% to 30%; for middle-agers, from 4% to 13%. When teen and middle-aged driving experience are examined in counties in which teen and middle-aged poverty rates each range from 8% to 14%, the fatality risk gap between teens and middle-agers narrows dramatically.

That is, *equalizing socioeconomic conditions shrinks the risk gap* between teen and adult drivers by 85%. In fact, under equal conditions, teens are no riskier than drivers over age 65 (29.5 fatal crashes per billion miles driven, poverty rates 8–14%). The most important factor predicting teen risk is driving experience, here operationalized as miles driven per day. Where teens drive a lot, they quickly improve—so much so that teens who drive a lot are actually safer on an absolute basis than teens who drive very little. A second, interrelated factor predicting low teen driving risk is low poverty and high income levels. Higher-income teens both drive more and are safer than low-income teen drivers—in fact, are at lower risk than older adults in high-risk counties.

Graduated Licensing

If experience and conditions are key factors in reducing risk, California's graduated licensing law (GDL) restricting teen drivers would not save lives. In fact, the only question is whether it has cost lives. Teenagers who began driving before the GDL law took effect have lower fatality rates by age 20 than teens who were subject to the law's restrictions. The reason is that *increased traffic death rates among 18–19 year-olds after the law more than offset lowered rates among 16–17 year-olds.* After the law took effect, traffic fatalities fell by 16% among 16–17 year-olds licensed under its restrictions. But this was more than offset by the 23% increase in fatalities when they later turned 18 and 19 compared to 18–19 year-old drivers licensed before the law took effect.

Overall, *traffic death rates rose by 7.1% among teens subjected to the law*, triple the 2.1% increase in traffic death rates among all California residents 16 and older during the same period. This represents a net teen fatality increase of 5% after rates are adjusted for population changes and changes in traffic death rates among all Californians 16 and older during the period. . . .

A Transition Period

A transition period from non-driver to driver status remains warranted, but not just for teens. The less experience a driver has, the greater his/her odds of being involved in traffic accidents per mile driven. However, new drivers who drive a lot under favorable conditions gain experience and become safer drivers remarkably rapidly—so much so that teens in high-driving counties have fatal accident rates far below those of teens in low-driving areas, and below those even of middle-aged drivers in many poorer counties. The question for policy makers is to balance the need to minimize the risks for novice drivers while allowing them to gain experience on the road.

Teenage drivers are far less dangerous, and the differences between teen and adult drivers much less extreme, than indicated in the inflamed rhetoric issued by commentators.

California's teen driving law should be changed to scrap the arbitrary, complicated, lengthy restrictions in favor of requiring all new drivers, regardless of age, to complete intensive on-the-road driver training by professional instructors, subsidized for low-income applicants. Research should focus on which real-life factors reduce the dangers experienced by new drivers, especially teens in wealthier counties who (despite their greater driving) have much lower fatality rates compared to those in poorer counties. . . .

A Commonsense Approach

Teenage drivers are far less dangerous, and the differences between teen and adult drivers much less extreme, than indicated in the inflamed rhetoric issued by commentators (including, unfortunately, a number described as "experts") in media stories and lobbying reports. Further, when examined in their full context, the risks posed by teen drivers (40% greater fatal crash rate per mile driven than the safest adult drivers under reasonably equalized conditions) are well within those society accepts for rare events. For example, male drivers are 77% more likely (per mile driven) to be in fatal crashes than are women drivers; doctors and lawyers as occupations are 95% more accident-prone than farmers and firefighters; drivers in Washington, DC, get into 140% more wrecks than drivers in Milwaukee; Mississippians and Montanans are 250% more at risk of fatal traffic accidents than residents of Connecticut and Massachusetts; drivers 75 and older suffer fatal crash rates 1.8 times those of middle-agers. Yet, evidencing the political power of adult age groups compared to teens, no one is proposing severely restricting or banning men, doctors, Southerners, or federal government officials and lobbyists from driving. Traffic safety measures should target risky conditions, not the political powerlessness of younger population groups.

Preventing teens from driving under realistic conditions brings more risks later as inexperienced drivers enter the adult driving world at age 18 or older. Learning to drive at ages 18–19 appears to entail more hazards than learning to drive at age 16, when family influences remain strong and the learning curve is more rapid. Both the safety of California's wealthier, heavy-driving teens, and the sharp increases in fatalities among 18–19 year-olds after the state's GDL restricted 16–17 year-olds, testify that it is not young age and immaturity, but poverty and lack of experience that raises teen driver risk. Put bluntly, the problem isn't adolescents' underdeveloped brains, but older generations' underdeveloped ethics in failing to share resources equitably to prevent youth poverty and in providing rationally-based transitions that allow youth to gain experience with adult behaviors.

Finally, more respectful, fair, and accurate treatment of teenagers in the press, by experts, and by institutions than is now afforded is crucial to establishing more sensible policies. *Researchers and experts should adopt higher standards for comparing teen and adult risks commensurate with those afforded when comparing adult population groups.* Media reporters should observe higher ethical standards when covering youth issues than simply featuring, in one-sided fashion, the most inflammatory allegations sources provide.

6

Graduated Licensing Restrictions for Teen Drivers Save Lives

Melissa A. Savage

Melissa Savage reports on safety issues for the National Conference of State Legislatures (NCSL), a bipartisan organization that provides research and technical assistance to U.S. state legislators and staffs and promotes the exchange of ideas on pressing state issues.

Driving license restrictions that limit the conditions under which teens may drive will reduce the risk teen drivers pose. The accident rate among inexperienced teen drivers is much higher than for other drivers, especially within the first year of driving. Laws that delay licensure until teens have supervised driving experience will therefore reduce the number of teen driving accidents. Since the fatal crash risk among teen drivers increases when teens drive at night and when distracted, laws that impose driving curfews, limit the number and ages of passengers, and prohibit cell phone use will save lives.

For teens, the license to drive is the key to freedom. The end of humiliating trips in the family van with mom or dad at the wheel. The end of waiting for a ride. The big step toward adulthood.

For parents, it's another kind of freedom. The end of carpooling and chauffeuring headaches. But it also is sleepless nights waiting for a young driver to come home.

Melissa A. Savage, "Surviving Driving," *State Legislatures*, February 2004, pp. 16–17. Copyright © 2004 National Conference of State Legislatures. Reproduced by permission.

The Price of Freedom

Each year 6,000 don't, and their parents live their worst nightmare: receiving the dreaded phone call telling them that their child has been killed in a crash. For 300,000 more parents each year, it means learning that their young driver has been injured.

Teens are more likely to speed and tailgate and less likely to wear seat belts than older drivers. It's no wonder accident rates for this age group are high. The National Safety Council reports that 20 percent of 16-year-old drivers will be involved in a crash at some point during their first year of driving—the accident rate is the highest during the first month. And 16-year-old drivers are three times more likely to end up in a wreck than older teens.

The big step toward adulthood comes with tremendous responsibility—and the need to make mature choices.

But teens are often ill-equipped to make the split-second decisions that can keep them safe on the road. Inexperience and immaturity behind the wheel is the leading cause of death for teens.

Times have changed. Now graduated driver's license laws appear to be saving young lives.

Crashes not only cause serious physical and emotional pain, they are costly. In 2001, car wrecks involving teen drivers cost tax-payers $42.3 billion for emergency services, medical and rehabilitation costs, productivity losses and property damage, according to the National Highway Traffic Safety Administration [NHTSA].

Once teens gain experience, they are safer and less likely to crash, studies show.

Times Have Changed

Until the mid-1990s, all it took for most teens to get their license was reaching their 16th birthday, a written exam and a road test. Teens were free to drive anywhere, any time with anyone. But times have changed. Now graduated driver's license laws appear to be saving young lives.

The Insurance Institute for Highway Safety [IIHS] recommends that states implement a learner's phase that begins at age 16, lasts at least six months and includes 30 to 50 hours of supervised driving. The group recommends an Intermediate phase that lasts until age 18 and includes a restriction on driving after 9 or 10 PM and no teen passengers in the car. Full licensure would be granted at 18.

[California's] teen passenger deaths decreased by 40 percent after its GDL [graduated driver's license] law went into effect.

Graduated driver's license (GDL) laws—even those that may be considered inadequate—do decrease accident rates for teen drivers. In Florida, fatality and injury accidents among 15- to 17-year-old drivers dropped after the law was adopted.

California saw a 23 percent decline in fatal and at-fault injury accidents for 16-year-olds. Teen passenger deaths decreased by 40 percent after its GDL law went into effect.

Curbing Teen Deaths

Traffic safety experts believe that restricting teen nighttime driving during the critical hours of 9 to 11 PM and limiting the number of teen passengers to only one, or ideally to none, are the best ways to curb deaths.

Reduced visibility, glare from oncoming traffic and fatigue make nighttime a challenge for all drivers, but especially for teens. The risk of being killed at night is especially high for beginning drivers—nearly three times higher than during the day for 16-year-olds—according to a study in the *Journal of Safety Research*. Restrictions that allow teens to drive at night with supervision lower the number of crashes during restricted hours by as much as 60 percent, the journal says.

North Carolina teens must be off the roads from 9 PM to 5 AM. Idaho restricts teen drivers from sunset to sunrise. In South Carolina, teen drivers aren't allowed on the roads from 6 PM to 6 AM.

Nighttime driving restrictions are not meant to be curfews, but rather to encourage supervised driving. "Most states already have curfews in place so teens shouldn't be out anyway," says Ashley Connors, Students Against Destructive Decisions [SADD] student of the year.

She also believes that these laws encourage teens to make better choices, which can be hard when faced with peer pressure. "If a law is in place, it's easier to say no to risky behavior. The law backs them up," she says.

Limiting Distractions

Maine and New Jersey recognize that young drivers talking on their cell phones are not focused on the road, so they have outlawed it for drivers under age 21.

Traffic safety advocates expect more states to pass similar laws in the future since studies have shown that new drivers are not able to drive safely and talk on the phone simultaneously.

Teen passengers pose another risk. Just one other teen in the car increases the crash risk by 50 percent, according to the Insurance Institute for Highway Safety. Three or more passengers increase the risk of a wreck by four times more than if the teen is driving alone.

California bans teens transporting anyone under the age of 20 for the first six months of their provisional licenses, unless accompanied by a parent or adult over 25. Teens can drive without supervision if the young passengers are family members, and a parent approves.

A 2003 Illinois law prohibits teens under 18 from driving with more than one passenger under age 20. Exceptions to the law include siblings and other family members. "This is a great bill," says Senator John Cullerton who sponsored it. "There was no organized opposition to it. And once suburban moms heard the statistics, they were supportive."

Although the Illinois bill faced little opposition, one in Maryland did. Sponsored by Delegate Adrienne Mandel, the bill would have prohibited drivers under 18 from transporting any teen passengers during the first six months of their provisional licenses. After that, they could drive with only one teen passenger until they turned 18. The bill was designed to restrict the "usual rolling party of seven, eight, nine teens crammed into a vehicle, and it's easy for police to enforce," says Mandel.

Opponents argued that restricting passengers would result in more teen drivers on the road. Others wanted exemptions for teenage family members to ride as passengers.

Delegate Mandel will introduce the bill again this session because "no GDL law is complete without a passenger restriction."

Traffic experts support the kinds of restrictions in graduated driver's license bills.

"Our objective is not to write more tickets, prohibit teens from driving or get in the way of family mobility," says Chuck Hurley, vice president of the National Safety Council. "We know how we can reduce crashes, injuries and fatalities. We know how we can save families and society money. We know how we can spare families, high schools and communities painful and numbing tragedies. And we should do that."

7

Current Graduated Licensing Restrictions for Teen Drivers Are Inadequate

Allan F. Williams

Allan F. Williams is a road safety consultant and former chief scientist at the Insurance Institute for Highway Safety, a research and communications organization funded by auto insurers.

While the graduated driver's licensing system has had some impact on reducing the teen crash rate, teen drivers continue to have a higher crash rate than older drivers. Policy makers must therefore extend the learner stage and toughen existing restrictions. Graduated licensing laws should require that learning drivers be supervised for at least six months. In addition, until teens are eighteen, they should not be allowed to drive after 9:00 PM. Moreover, teen drivers should only be allowed to carry one teen passenger. The safety of those on America's roads should override any inconvenience these restrictions may pose.

Every motorized country in the world has a young driver problem. In the United States, licensing practices in place for most of the 20th century exacerbated the problem. Licensing ages around the world vary from 15 to 18, for example, but in the United States they are at the low end of this range. There also has been a quick and easy path to licensure, with minimal requirements and easy tests. Thus until recent years

Allan F. Williams, "Next Step for Graduated Licensing," *Traffic Injury Prevention*, vol. 6, September, 2005, pp. 119–201. Copyright © 2005 Taylor & Francis, Inc. Reproduced by permission of Taylor & Francis, Ltd., http//:www.tandf.co.uk/journals, conveyed through Copyright Clearance Center, and the author.

there was little attempt to address the two main factors creating the problem: inexperience and youthful age. The result was a young driver problem of epidemic proportions.

The Impact of Graduated Licensing

This picture began to change in the late 1990s as states adopted graduated licensing, a system for phasing in young beginners to full driving privileges and protecting them while they acquire initial on-road driving experience. An extended learner stage provides opportunity for practice driving under adult supervision. Once licensed, restrictions initially are imposed on high risk driving—late at night and driving with young passengers. Night restrictions had existed in a few states prior to the mid-1990s but were unpopular when proposed in the 1970s and 1980s. For reasons not fully understood, graduated licensing became enormously popular. As of early 2005, 37 states plus the District of Columbia [D.C.] have three-stage systems—that is, an extended learner period and restrictions on high-risk driving upon licensure, followed by full licensure. Several other states adopted single elements of graduated licensing during this period, typically an extended learner phase.

State evaluations typically have reported crash reductions of 20–30% for affected age groups, primarily 16 year-olds, the main targets. Nationally, fatal crash rates for 16-year-old drivers have fallen significantly.

With most states having enacted some legislation, Phase I of graduated licensing is basically over. Fifteen states have strengthened their original laws, and additional legislation is anticipated. However, little action occurred during 2003–2004, so the graduated licensing movement appears to be winding down. It would be unfortunate if attention to the young driver problem shifts after this initial legislative flurry. In Canada, where most provinces have adopted graduated systems during the past decade, a recent public opinion poll found that "the majority of Canadian drivers are not concerned about young driver safety."

Although the young driver problem has been reduced, it still is a major concern.

A Continuing Concern

The question is: Where do we go from here? This is important because although the young driver problem has been reduced, it still is a major concern. In 2003, 16-year-old drivers still had a higher crash rate per licensed driver compared with any other age group, more than four times the rate for drivers ages 20 and older.

An outbreak of teenage crash deaths in late 2004 in the D.C. area—18 deaths in 11 weeks—provides another illustration of the remaining problem. All three local jurisdictions— D.C., Maryland, and Virginia—have three-stage graduated systems, with D.C. and Virginia being 2 of only 16 jurisdictions the Insurance Institute for Highway Safety (2004) rates as having "good" systems. The rash of teenage deaths aroused great public concern and clearly indicates that continued attention is needed.

We know why the problem exists. Driver mistakes can have lethal consequences, and driver inexperience increases the likelihood of mistakes. Risk increases when beginners are at the stage of adolescence where risk taking is a normative feature and brain development is at a stage at which controls on risk taking are not fully in place. Peer influences also can increase risk. Clearly there is a continuum of age-associated risk; not all adolescents are equally vulnerable. However, it is not the case that "good" kids are spared, and the recent D.C. area teenage deaths provide several examples of this.

There are two main ways to make further progress in the United States. One is to delay licensure; the other is to provide additional protected experience. Both of these goals can be accomplished through graduated licensing, building on existing legislation. It is time for Phase II of graduated licensing.

Delaying Licensure

There are various ways to delay licensure. One is simply to raise the licensing age to 17 or 18. In some countries, licensing exams are very tough and very expensive, which inhibits and delays licensure. This likely would not be a very popular approach in the United States, and raising the licensing age to 17 or higher—though sometimes suggested—has never been considered seriously by legislators in any state. The licensing age in New Jersey, however, has been 17 for many years.

> *The amount of protected driving experience . . . can be maximized by both extending the learner stage and toughening the restrictions governing initial licensed driving.*

However, licensure delay can and is being achieved through graduated licensing, which can increase the age at which learner's permits are obtained and extend learner stage requirements. For example, in Kentucky, where licenses are permitted at age 16, learner's permits cannot be obtained until age 16. Before graduated licensing, a license could be obtained a month after the 16th birthday; but with the addition of a minimum holding period of 6 months, licensing is delayed until at least 16 years, 6 months. Connecticut and a few other states have a similar feature, and both Connecticut and Kentucky have reported large reductions in 16-year-old crash involvements. Other states could make similar gains by raising the permit age to 16 and/or further extending the minimum learner stage, which also would allow for accumulation of additional protected driving experience. More modest shifts in the minimum permit age also can delay licensure. For ex-

E.O. Smith Library Media Center

ample, California recently raised the permit age from 15 to 15 years, 6 months. A permit must be held for at least 6 months, and a license can be obtained at age 16. This change can be expected to produce an increase in the age at which California teenagers get their licenses.

Maximizing Experience

The amount of protected driving experience gained in a graduated system can be maximized by both extending the learner stage and toughening the restrictions governing initial licensed driving. Studies around the world have found the supervised learner stage to be quite safe. However, upon licensure crash risk increases dramatically then decreases during the next few months. This risk profile is thought to be related largely to driving experience. The unique feature of graduated licensing is to keep new license holders out of the very highest risk situations during this vulnerable period, thus encouraging the accumulation of mileage in lower risk settings. However, nighttime and passenger restrictions are absent or weak in many states. Thirty-eight states have night driving restrictions, but 23 of them do not start until midnight or 1 AM, thus bypassing the high-risk late evening hours when the majority of nighttime crashes occur. In 2003, 62% of fatal crashes and 78% of all crashes occurring during the 9 PM–5 AM period took place before midnight. Fewer states (27) have passenger restrictions, and several of these restrictions allow as many as three passengers, known to be a very high-risk scenario for young drivers.

No state has put all of the rules together for a comprehensive graduated system.

No state has what would be considered an excellent system—a minimum learner age of 16, a required learner holding period of at least 6 months, a nighttime restriction start-

E.O. Smith Library Media Center

ing at 9 PM, and a restriction allowing no more than one young passenger, with both nighttime and passenger restrictions in force until age 18. These roles are not beyond reach. Each of them exists in several states, but no state has put all of the rules together for a comprehensive graduated system.

A Need for Adjustments

Besides these changes, other adjustments are needed. Some licensing systems have features that hamper their effectiveness. For example, in Kentucky there is the illogical combination of a restriction on late night practice driving in the learner stage but no such restriction upon licensure. And in many states in which driver education is optional, beginners who complete courses are given special privileges—for example, shorter learner periods or being allowed to drive during restricted nighttime hours at an earlier age. This defeats the purpose of graduated licensing, and because driver education is well known not to produce safer drivers, it is not justified.

Graduated licensing laws can be modified in other ways. For example, seat belt use generally is lower among teenage drivers and passengers than adults. North Carolina has explicit belt use requirements and penalties in its graduated system, requiring belt use by all vehicle occupants, and provides a model for other states. Three jurisdictions (D.C., Maine, and New Jersey) have banned cell phone use for drivers in the graduated system. New Jersey also applies its graduated licensing law to older novices, except that the nighttime and passenger restrictions are waived for new drivers 21 and older. The typical practice is to cover only drivers younger than 18, who are the highest risk beginners, but older novices also have heightened crash risk.

The Importance of Compliance

Strong laws are the foundation of graduated licensing, but compliance is key to effectiveness. This is an issue with late night restrictions and particularly passenger restrictions. Research is proceeding on ways to get parents more involved in the licensing process and in enforcing existing rules and creating their own. A model program is being tried in North Carolina to get police more involved in enforcing graduated licensing rules. Focus groups have indicated that parents understand they are the primary enforcers, but they want police involved to validate and bolster their efforts.

The young driver problem is a focus of attention in Europe and Australia/New Zealand. A comprehensive report on young drivers and injury prevention strategies is being prepared by the Organization for Economic Cooperation and Development. An international perspective reveals that among the approaches countries are taking to address this issue, graduated licensing is arguably the most effective.

Newspaper headlines about the teenage deaths in the D.C. area included "Sweet 16: Not for Driving—Teen Death Rates Call for Decisive Action" and "As Dreams Die Young, Answers Are Elusive." Actually the answers are not elusive. Graduated licensing has proven to be popular and successful in the United States; extending it would achieve further substantial gains. These would come at the expense of some mobility, and societies have to decide where they want to strike the balance between mobility for young people and safety concerns for everyone on the road, including the teenagers. This is not necessarily an obvious choice. The implementation of Phase II of graduated licensing depends on how seriously society takes the problem of deaths and injuries associated with young drivers.

8

Driver Education Does Not Improve Teen Driving Safety

Allan F. Williams and Susan A. Ferguson

Allan F. Williams is a road safety consultant and former chief scientist at the Insurance Institute for Highway Safety (IIHS). Susan A. Ferguson is senior vice president for research at IIHS, a research and communications organization funded by auto insurers.

Evidence shows that pre-license driver training does not reduce the number of teen driving accidents. In fact, driver education may actually increase the number of teen crashes. Because teens that complete driver education often get their licenses earlier, such programs can result in a greater number of young, inexperienced drivers on America's roads and an increase in the number of teen car crashes. Despite this evidence, driver education continues to garner public support. Since resources are scarce and driver education is proven to be ineffective, these resources should be put to better use.

Despite decades of research indicating driver education does not reduce crash involvement among beginning drivers, it still has tremendous popular appeal as a means to improve driver safety. Formal driver education programs enjoy widespread public acceptance around the world as the preferred way to prepare beginners for licensure. For example, a survey in the United States found that 86% considered driver

Allan F. Williams and Susan A. Ferguson, "Driver Education Renaissance? Why We Need Evidence Based Highway Safety Policy," *Injury Prevention*, vol. 10, February 2004, pp. 4–7. Copyright © 2004 British Medical Association. Reproduced by permission. Title and headings have been added by Cengage.

education courses "very important" in training new drivers to drive safely. Only 2% thought it was not important. When the young driver problem is addressed in public forums, there inevitably is an appeal for more or better driver education.

There is no difference in the crash records of driver education graduates compared with equivalent groups of beginners who learned to drive without formal education.

Evaluating Driver Education

Several comprehensive international reviews of the best scientific evaluations of driver education programs for young beginners all come to the same conclusion: There is no difference in the crash records of driver education graduates compared with equivalent groups of beginners who learned to drive without formal education. The [2001] review of driver education studies [by R. Christie] states, "There is little evidence that pre-license training per se reduces crash rates among novice drivers in the short or longer term.". . .

There is little reason to think driver education should produce drivers less likely to crash. The courses generally are of short duration (for example, 30 hours in-class and six hours in-vehicle); in the available time, it is possible to teach only basic driving skills. There is less opportunity to teach safe driving techniques, and any safety messages that are conveyed can be overwhelmed by ongoing parental, peer, personal, and other social influences that shape driving styles and crash involvement. Such influences largely are beyond the reach of driver education instructors. For the same reasons, many short term high school health education programs aimed at influencing smoking, alcohol, and other drug use have failed, although programs that are comprehensive and longer term, targeting the entire community, have had some success. The audience for driver education courses also may be relatively unmotivated by safety concerns. In surveys, most teenagers say they want to get licensed as soon as possible, and the goal of many driver education students is likely to center on learning enough skills to pass the driving test. Developmental and lifestyle features typical of young adolescents (risk taking, feelings of invulnerability, immature decision making) also make it difficult to influence the way they drive through safety messages. . . .

An Unclear Contribution

What, then, is pre-license driver education able to contribute? In a 1977 article, Pat Waller discussed the unrealistic expectations of a high school driver education teacher, compared with the way teachers of other subjects are judged. She asked the question, "Should the driver education teacher be responsible only for whether the student can drive adequately or whether he actually does drive in this manner?" and went on to note the many outside factors that influence subsequent driving performance.

[Driver education] is associated with early licensure, which leads to additional crashes and injuries.

It seems apparent that driver education should be considered as one method for teaching young beginners how to drive adequately, that is, it is a way to learn basic driving skills. Is it the best method? Driver education courses vary, so there is no blanket answer. However, one would expect professional instruction to be superior to lay instruction for teaching skills, and there is some evidence that good programs accomplish this. For example, the Safe Performance Curriculum group in the landmark DeKalb County [Georgia] study received what was considered at the time to be state of the art driver education, and this group scored higher on the Southern California on-road performance test than those in a control group or minimum training group.

The Effects of Driver Education

It would be more defensible if driver education were promoted as the best way to learn driving skills rather than as a way to produce safer drivers. However, driver education is not benign. When available at early ages, it is associated with earlier licensure, which leads to additional crashes and injuries. This finding has been reported in several studies in the United States. Many states in the United States require driver education as a condition of licensure before age 18, so this is one way driver education leads to early licensure (although licensure can be delayed if driver education courses are hard to come by). However, independent of driver education requirements, the easy availability of driver education has been found to lead to earlier licensure in both states where it is optional and states where it is required. The strength of this relationship was demonstrated when some Connecticut high schools dropped driver education, which led to a 75% decline in licensure among 16–17 year olds and a substantial decline in crashes.

The relationship between driver education and early licensure also has been reported in studies in Australia, Canada, England, and New Zealand. Earlier licensure enhances mobility, which has important benefits for teenagers, but at the expense of safety.

Here is how [Christie's] review of the international driver education literature summarizes the situation:

> The research literature suggests that, beyond imparting basic car control and road law knowledge skills, pre-license driver training/education contributes little to post-license reductions in casualty crashes or traffic violations among novice drivers. In addition, mandatory pre-license training or even formal pre-license training/education, such as high school driver education programs in the USA, may contribute to increased exposure-to-risk for young drivers, particularly females, by encouraging early solo licensing. There is also

considerable evidence that driver training that attempts to impart advanced skills such as skid control to learner drivers may contribute to increased crash risk, particularly among young males. This pattern of results has been confirmed and replicated across numerous studies conducted in Australia, New Zealand, North America, Europe and Scandinavia during the last 30 years.

Despite the scientific evidence that driver education has neutral or negative effects, it has enduring appeal.

Some licensing systems include provisions that implicitly assume driver education graduates are safer drivers. The results are detrimental. For example, some jurisdictions in Canada, the United States, and New Zealand allow beginners with driver education to spend less time in the learner stage of graduated licensing systems. Two states in the United States allow earlier graduation from the late night driving restriction for initial license holders. These time discounts are contrary to graduated licensing principles, which are based on time in the system, and have compromised the overall positive effects of graduated systems. In Nova Scotia, the learner phase can be reduced from six to three months with driver education. Novices who took advantage of this time discount had a crash rate when first licensed that was 27% higher than newly licensed drivers without driver education. In Ontario, where the learner period can be reduced from 12 to eight months, novices with driver education had a crash rate when first licensed that was 44% higher than those who did not take driver education. The reasons for these differences are not clear but may be related to amounts of exposure. These are not direct tests of the effects of driver education because young drivers self selected whether they would take the course. However, the findings provide a strong argument against special privileges for driver education graduates.

The Enduring Appeal of Driver Education

Despite the scientific evidence that driver education has neutral or negative effects, it has enduring appeal and continues to be sold and promoted on the basis that it enhances safety. Several recent examples illustrate this appeal. In 2000, the British government launched its road safety plan, which included a large component of driver education. After reviewing the research literature, the Cochrane Review Group unsuccessfully protested this development because of concern that "the government's road safety strategy included an intervention that may increase teenage road traffic crashes."

In 2003 Ford Motor Company, in concert with the National Highway Traffic Safety Administration and with the involvement of many major safety organizations in the United States, launched "Real World Driver: Driving Skills for Life", which involves the distribution of educational materials to every public high school (more than 20,000) across the United States. The accompanying press release stated that "most of the crashes and resulting injuries and deaths could be prevented if teenagers better understood the necessary skills for safely driving vehicles." Decades of research suggest this statement is false.

In the case of the pre-license driver education, there is a major discrepancy between public beliefs and scientific knowledge.

In October 2003, the National Transportation Safety Board convened a two day public forum to "explore the strengths and weaknesses of driver education programs and what can be done to improve them."

Another example involves BMW. In June 2003, this company introduced a free, nationwide student driving program. The half day course featured instruction in skid control and emergency recovery—that is, instruction that has been shown by research to increase the crash problem.

Driver education is constantly reinventing itself, and several new programs have been developed recently in the United States, Europe, Australia, and New Zealand. These programs are thoughtfully and carefully planned, but they have not been evaluated. Given the formidable barriers to making young beginners safer drivers through education and training and the disappointing results of prior evaluations of programs initially thought to be excellent, it is essential to scientifically evaluate new programs before fully launching them. . . .

Reducing Crash Risk Is Key

In the case of pre-license driver education, there is a major discrepancy between public beliefs and scientific knowledge. There is wide public support for programs that, in fact, do not produce safer drivers and can have unintended negative consequences. Of considerable concern is that scarce resources continue to be spent in the name of safety on programs that have no benefit or may even make things worse. In such a case, the wisest course would be to blunt the harmful effects of driver education and redirect it in ways that take advantage of what it can do (that is, teach basic driving skills). Many new approaches are being tried or are under development, but they should not be widely applied unless rigorous assessments indicate they are effective in reducing crash risk.

9

Driver Education Lays a Foundation for Safe Teen Driving Skills

David C. Huff

David C. Huff is director of the Traffic Safety Program in Montana's Office of Public Instruction.

Current research indicates that teens who complete standards-based driver education programs are safer drivers. Indeed, the American public continues to support funding for driver education programs. Nevertheless, critics want to divert these funds to promote graduated driver models that focus on increasing the quantity of teen driving experience. However, the quantity of driving experience alone is insufficient to develop safe driving skills. Those who understand how teens learn know that teens must be taught safe driving behaviors from skilled driver education instructors.

Why do some research professionals continue to hold positions that result in avoiding a serious overhaul of, and investment into, educating new drivers? Education-testing young drivers warrants as much attention and investment as crash-testing new vehicles! Exploring how to teach and motivate teen drivers will result in knowledge that is likely more valuable to society and traffic safety than exploring the crush of a new vehicle!

Researchers Allan Williams and Susan Ferguson of the Insurance Institute for Highway Safety (IIHS) have weighed in

David C. Huff, "A Rebuttal to Skeptics of Teen Driver Education," *Chronicle of the American Driver & Traffic Safety Education Association*, vol. 53, Spring, 2005, p. 306. Reproduced by permission.

once again on their position regarding driver education. Although they title their article "Driver's Education Renaissance?", their comments reflect an old position that does not promote education; it promotes delaying and avoiding education. The premise of this position is kids who don't drive won't crash, and educating someone on how to do something will result in them doing it. . . . This article is a rebuttal to the position they put forward.

An Attack on Driver Education

This author found no positive suggestions for improving driver education in the Williams and Ferguson commentary, yet research abounds on how people learn, and the body of knowledge on how it applies to driver education, although still largely ignored, continues to grow. Their specific, useful positive suggestions are limited to the agreed benefits of various elements of graduated driver experience models. But, because driver education results in kids driving, they also recommend that access to driver education be made less convenient by removing it from high schools.

Most parents and teachers believe education is important to help teens learn safe driving behaviors.

Those who would define the agenda on teen driver education should be able to offer something more positive than to make driver education less convenient to the general public. This suggestion leads this author to believe they are at a loss on how to improve driver education, or as to what role it can provide in improving the learning experiences of young drivers.

Their commentary continues their public message that scarce public dollars will be wasted if spent on driver education. They disclose that a good driver education program results in more skilled drivers, but the context and underlying message is "skilled drivers are not necessarily safe drivers." Even so, the article also conveys the fact that efforts over the past couple decades to convince the public that education measures are useless have failed, and with that admission the article appears to divulge a concern that efforts to keep public dollars from being invested into driver education are at risk.

The Williams and Ferguson article appears to be part of a strategy, perhaps well intended, to counter the ongoing struggle to adequately fund and improve driver education—a counter stimulated by renewed interest of the public and Congress in driver education. The struggle that exists between some researchers and those who directly work with teens is a challenging conundrum. Most parents and teachers believe education is important to help teens learn safe driving behaviors, but some of those who review literature and research at arms length from young, aspiring drivers believe teens should not be taught to do something that might result in their harm.

Emerging reports . . . indicate teens whose learning experience includes a standards-based, state-approved driver education program are safer drivers.

Would Williams or Ferguson consider delaying young minds from being taught the basics of the scientific method? Any teacher can tell you that young minds will error in their methods, analysis and conclusions until they learn, through experience, to master the skill. Yet, society knows that young minds should be taught. Teachers, therefore, work patiently, over time, to establish a foundation of knowledge in the scientific method and provide expanding experience, helping students overcome errors and produce more accurate conclusions in more complex scientific inquiries. Society demands this be done because society understands the value of the educational process.

Countering the Critics

The facts cited by Williams and Ferguson overlook new emerging reports coming out of Washington and Oregon that indicate teens whose learning experience includes a standards-based, state-approved driver education program are safer drivers than those who do not take a state-approved driver education program. In addition, what is known by research is not the only useful body of knowledge relating to teen drivers. The writers report "86 percent" of the public "considered driver education courses 'very important' in training new drivers to drive safely." Those who are closer to the real world have ways of understanding things that frustrate the analytical and necessarily myopic world of research and empiricism. We must respect what is unscientifically "known" by the public. In fact, intuitive knowledge and hunches are an important seedbed of hypotheses that eventually become scientific knowledge.

Champions and guardians of empirical knowledge are invaluable contributors to public discussion and policy development. However, I learned years ago that while the advice of accountants and researchers is very important, unless those analyzing the data understand the heartbeat of the business, their advice may not result in the hoped for outcome. Why is that? It is because the world of science is a discovery process and what has been empirically explored and documented represents only the tiniest piece of the universe of knowledge awaiting exploration. Despite our great and wonderful advances, what is unknown is far greater than what is known, and what is thought to be known is often, at best, only partially known.

It is not unusual for researchers to warn that a particular effort represents a focus for which there is no scientifically proven value, only to find through additional research that there is evidence of its value. Examples of this abound.

The Best Use of Resources

Delaying licenses may reduce crashes for the younger teens, but what does it do for the older teens who have yet to learn to drive, and how does that help rural states that insist on young teens being able to drive? At some point the would-be driver must learn to drive and begin the path of acquiring experience. Society has invested too little effort and resources into improving methods of initial instruction. The public intuitively knows that education has to play a part as certainly as the staff at the IIHS know that young minds must be taught the scientific method.

A quality driver education and training experience is the foundation for safe driving behavior.

Perhaps the driver education agenda should be defined by experts in education, learning development and human behavior who have explored the nuances of the human mind and know the heartbeat of the education and training process. Perhaps it's time to expand the dialogue to folks who have suggestions other than Williams' and Ferguson's suggestion to avoid or delay the task, and who are willing to forge ahead and improve a driver education system that has yet to embrace present education and training knowledge and technologies. Perhaps experts at crashing cars and calculating the costs of crashes for insurance companies are not the experts that can best advance solutions to the driver education challenges.

The bottom line is that experience without skilled and knowledgeable instruction will lead to reinforcement and establishment of poor and illegal driving behaviors and habits. Society can't expect the teen driver to drive safely if they do not know how. A quality driver education and training experience is the foundation for safe driving behavior. That foundation needs to be true and sound so that subsequent safe-driver initiatives can build upon that foundation of knowledge and skill, including public policies that encourage improved driving norms for all drivers.

In the words of Russell W. Davenport, "Progress in every age results only from the fact that there are some men and women who refuse to believe that what they know to be right cannot be done."

10

The Driving Age Should Be Increased

Robert Davis

Robert Davis is a staff writer for USA Today.

A growing number of Americans believe that increasing the driving age would reduce the epidemic of fatal teen-driving accidents. Many brain researchers and safety experts agree. Mounting evidence reveals, for example, that a sixteen-year-old brain is not completely developed. When teens are speeding their brain's thrill center is working perfectly but the part of their brain that weighs risks is not yet fully developed. Since a record number of teens will soon be driving, the time to increase the driving age and avert fatal car crashes is now.

R aise the driving age. That radical idea is gaining momentum in the fight to save the lives of teenage drivers—the most dangerous on the USA's roads—and their passengers.

Brain and auto safety experts fear that 16-year-olds, the youngest drivers licensed in most states, are too immature to handle today's cars and roadway risks.

New findings from brain researchers at the National Institutes of Health [NIH] explain for the first time why efforts to protect the youngest drivers usually fail. The weak link: what's called "the executive branch" of the teen brain—the part that weighs risks, makes judgments and controls impulsive behavior.

Robert Davis, "Is 16 Too Young to Drive a Car?" *www.USAToday.com*, March 2, 2005. Copyright 2005, *USA Today*. Reprinted with permission.

Scientists at the NIH campus in Bethesda, Md., have found that this vital area develops through the teenage years and isn't fully mature until age 25. One 16-year-old's brain might be more developed than another 18-year-old's, just as a younger teen might be taller than an older one. But evidence is mounting that a 16-year-old's brain is generally far less developed than those of teens just a little older.

Studies have convinced a growing number of safety experts that 16-year-olds are too young to drive safely without supervision.

The research seems to help explain why 16-year-old drivers crash at far higher rates than older teens. The studies have convinced a growing number of safety experts that 16-year-olds are too young to drive safely without supervision.

"Privately, a lot of people in safety think it's a good idea to raise the driving age," says Barbara Harsha, executive director of the Governors Highway Safety Association. "It's a topic that is emerging."

Public Opinion

Americans increasingly favor raising the driving age, a *USA TODAY*/CNN/Gallup Poll has found. Nearly two-thirds—61%—say they think a 16-year-old is too young to have a driver's license. Only 37% of those polled thought it was OK to license 16-year-olds, compared with 50% who thought so in 1995.

A slight majority, 53%, think teens should be at least 18 to get a license.

The poll of 1,002 adults, conducted Dec. 17–19, 2004, has an error margin of +/-3 percentage points.

Many states have begun to raise the age by imposing restrictions on 16-year-old drivers. Examples: limiting the number of passengers they can carry or barring late-night driving.

But the idea of flatly forbidding 16-year-olds to drive without parental supervision—as New Jersey does—has run into resistance from many lawmakers and parents around the country.

Irving Slosberg, a Florida state representative who lost his 14-year-old daughter in a 1995 crash, says that when he proposed a law to raise the driving age, other lawmakers "laughed at me."

Bill Van Tassel, AAA's [American Automobile Association's] national manager of driving training programs, hears both sides of the argument. "We have parents who are pretty much tired of chauffeuring their kids around, and they want their children to be able to drive," he says. "Driving is a very emotional issue."

But safety experts fear inaction could lead to more young lives lost. Some sound a note of urgency about changing course. The reason: A record number of American teenagers will soon be behind the wheel as the peak of the "baby boomlet" hits driving age.

Teen Driving Fatalities

Already, on average, two people die every day across the USA in vehicles driven by 16-year-old drivers. One in five 16-year-olds will have a reportable car crash within the first year.

In 2003, there were 937 drivers age 16 who were involved in fatal crashes. In those wrecks, 411 of the 16-year-old drivers died and 352 of their passengers were killed. Sixteen-year-old drivers are involved in fatal crashes at a rate nearly five times the rate of drivers 20 or older.

Gayle Bell, whose 16-year-old daughter, Jessie, rolled her small car into a Missouri ditch and died in July 2003, says she used to happily be Jessie's "ride." She would give anything for the chance to drive Jessie again.

"We were always together, but not as much after she got her license," Bell says. "If I could bring her back, I'd lasso the moon."

Most states have focused their fixes on giving teens more driving experience before granting them unrestricted licenses. But the new brain research suggests that a separate factor is just as crucial: maturity. A new 17- or 18-year-old driver is considered safer than a new 16-year-old driver.

Even some teens are acknowledging that 16-year-olds are generally not ready to face the life-threatening risks that drivers can encounter behind the wheel.

"Raising the driving age from 16 to 17 would benefit society as a whole," says Liza Darwin, 17, of Nashville. Though many parents would be inconvenienced and teens would be frustrated, she says, "It makes sense to raise the driving age to save more lives."

The Lawmakers

But those in a position to raise the driving age—legislators in states throughout the USA—have mostly refused to do so.

Adrienne Mandel, a Maryland state legislator, has tried since 1997 to pass tougher teen driving laws. Even lawmakers who recognize that a higher driving age could save lives, Mandel notes, resist the notion of having to drive their 16-year-olds to after-school activities that the teens could drive to themselves.

Among the general public, majorities in both suburbs (65%) and urban areas (60%) favor licensing ages above 16.

"Other delegates said, 'What are you doing? You're going to make me drive my kid to the movies on Friday night for another six months?'" Mandel says. "Parents are talking about inconvenience, and I'm talking about saving lives."

Yet the *USA TODAY* poll found that among the general public, majorities in both suburbs (65%) and urban areas (60%) favor licensing ages above 16.

While a smaller percentage in rural areas (54%) favor raising the driving age, experts say it's striking that majority support exists even there, considering that teens on farms often start driving very young to help with workloads.

For those who oppose raising the minimum age, their argument is often this: Responsible teen drivers shouldn't be punished for the mistakes of the small fraction who cause deadly crashes.

The debate stirs images of reckless teens drag-racing or driving drunk. But such flagrant misdeeds account for only a small portion of the fatal actions of 16-year-old drivers. Only about 10% of the 16-year-old drivers killed in 2003 had blood-alcohol concentrations of 0.10 or higher, compared with 43% of 20- to 49-year-old drivers killed, according to the Insurance Institute for Highway Safety.

Instead, most fatal crashes with 16-year-old drivers (77%) involved driver errors, especially the kind most common among novices. Examples: speeding, overcorrecting after veering off the road, and losing control when facing a roadway obstacle that a more mature driver would be more likely to handle safely. That's the highest percentage of error for any age group.

For years, researchers suspected that inexperience—the bane of any new driver—was mostly to blame for deadly crashes involving teens. When trouble arose, the theory went, the young driver simply made the wrong move. But in recent years, safety researchers have noticed a pattern emerge—one that seems to stem more from immaturity than from inexperience.

"Skills are a minor factor in most cases," says Allan Williams, former chief scientist at the insurance institute. "It's really attitudes and emotions."

A Peek Inside the Brain

The NIH brain research suggests that the problem is human biology. A crucial part of the teen's brain—the area that peers ahead and considers consequences—remains undeveloped. That means careless attitudes and rash emotions often drive teen decisions, says Jay Giedd, chief of brain imaging in the child psychiatric unit at the National Institute of Mental Health, who's leading the study.

"It all comes down to impulse control," Giedd says. "The brain is changing a lot longer than we used to think. And that part of the brain involved in decision-making and controlling impulses is among the latest to come on board.". . .

When a teen is traveling 15 to 20 miles per hour over the speed limit, the part of his or her brain that processes a thrill is working brilliantly. But the part that warns of negative consequences? It's all but useless.

"It may not seem that fast to them," Giedd says, because they're not weighing the same factors an adult might. They're not asking themselves, he says, "'Should I go fast or not?' And dying is not really part of the equation.". . .

Finding Explanations

The new insights into the teen brain might help explain why efforts to protect young drivers, ranging from driver education to laws that restrict teen driving, have had only modest success. With the judgment center of the teen brain not fully developed, parents and states must struggle to instill decision-making skills in still-immature drivers.

In nearly every state, 16-year-old drivers face limits known as "graduated licensing" rules. These restrictions vary. But typically, they bar 16-year-olds from carrying other teen passengers, driving at night or driving alone until they have driven a certain number of hours under parental supervision.

These states have, in effect, already raised their driving age. Safety experts say lives have been saved as a result. But it's mostly left to parents to enforce the restrictions, and the evidence suggests enforcement has been weak.

Teens probably appear to their parents at the dinner table to be more in control than they are behind the wheel. They might recite perfectly the risks of speeding, drinking and driving or distractions, such as carrying passengers or talking on a cell phone, Giedd says. But their brains are built to learn more from example.

For teenagers, years of watching parents drive after downing a few glasses of wine or while chatting on a cell phone might make a deeper imprint than a lecture from a driver education teacher.

The brain research raises this question: How well can teen brains respond to the stresses of driving?

More research on teen driving decisions is needed, safety advocates say, before definitive conclusions can be drawn. And more public support is probably needed before politicians would seriously consider raising the driving age.

11

The Driving Age Should Not Be Increased

Allen Robinson

Allen Robinson is chief executive officer of the American Driver and Traffic Safety Education Association (ADTSEA), a professional association that represents traffic safety educators. ADTSEA is a national advocate for quality traffic safety education.

Calls to increase the driving age are an overreaction to misleading statistics on the risks of teen driving. While raising the driving age might reduce the number of sixteen-year-old drivers killed, it would do nothing to reduce the number of teen drivers killed each year overall. In addition, preventing all sixteen-year-olds from driving due to the tragic deaths of a minority of teens is unfair. Rather than increase the driving age, the more logical solution is to enforce current restrictions and better train all teens to drive safely.

[M]any] have read the [March 2005] series of articles in *USA Today* concerning teen traffic deaths. As we all know, this is a problem that requires many solutions. Unfortunately, the writers and contributors to these stories believe the quick fix is to change the licensing age to 17 or 18 years of age. It is obvious that if you don't drive, you will not be killed as a driver, but it doesn't change the high probability of dying as a passenger.

Misleading Readers

The problem with statistics and reporting of statistics is that writers mislead the reader. Highway fatalities are a grave con-

Allen Robinson, "ADTSEA's Response to *USA Today*," *American Driver & Traffic Safety Education Association*. Reproduced by permission. http://adtsea.iup.edu.

cern to all of us. Using statistics inaccurately to push a cause does not solve the problem. Most researchers and traffic safety professionals illustrate the statistical problem associated with teen drivers. As an example, the Insurance Institute for Highway Safety [IIHS] reports that [among] motor vehicle crash deaths per 100,000 people in 2003, the 16 to 19 age group had a death rate of 29.1. This same year the 20 to 24 age group had a death rate of 27.0 and males in this age group had a higher death rate than males in the 16 to 19 age group.

This special report in *USA Today* also reports that 1 in 5 16-year-olds crash their cars within the first year. This also means that 4 in 5 16-year-olds do not crash.

The headline in the *USA Today* on March 1, 2005 was "Deadly Teen Auto Crashes Show a Pattern. The most dangerous drivers: 16-year-olds and most deadly single vehicle teen crashes involve night driving or at least one passenger 16 to 19." On the front of Section B the following question is asked: "Is 16 too young to drive a car?" *USA Today* Poll found: 3 in 5 say 16-years-old is too young to have a license. Another headline read: "On an average day, 10 teens are killed in teen driven autos." In 2003 *USA Today* reports that 3,500 teenagers died in traffic crashes.

[USA Today's] solution of raising the driving age makes little sense.

Missing the Point

All of these statistics when used in context are correct. However, when the researchers and the writers say that the solution to the teen fatality problem is to raise the legal driving age, they are missing the point. In 2003 there were 937 16-year-old drivers killed in traffic crashes. This new driving age does nothing for the other 2,563 teens killed in 2003.

This series of articles did not mention the number of 16-year-old individuals in the U.S. population. According to the U.S. Census Bureau there were 3,975,021 16-year-olds in 2000. An estimate for 2003 is 4,010,850. The Insurance Institute reports that 31 percent of the 16-year-olds received driver licenses in 2003. The Federal Highway Administration—Highway Statistics 2003 reports that 1,262,899 16-year-olds were licensed to drive in 2003. By comparing these figures we see they do agree.

In 2003 there were 937 16-year-olds killed in teen crashes. Does it seem realistic to prevent 1,262,899 16-year-olds from obtaining a driver's license that will assist them with opportunities to: go to school, participate in extracurricular school activities, go to work and be involved in other social activities? Their solution of raising the driving age makes little sense.

The solution is not preventing license use, but to better train and use stricter licensing tests before issuing a driver's license to a 16-year-old or any new driver. Training does not exist today for most teenagers who desire a driver's license. When training is available, it is often inadequate. We need to look at the real problem and not the confusing statistical analysis of critics of young drivers.

12

Teen Driving Improves When Parents and Teens Agree on Rules

Kenneth H. Beck, Jessica L. Hartos, and Bruce G. Simons-Morton

Kenneth H. Beck is a professor of public and community health at the University of Maryland; Jessica L. Hartos is an assistant professor in the Department of Health Behavior and Administration, University of North Carolina; Bruce G. Simons-Morton is with the Prevention Research Branch of the National Institute of Child Health and Human Development, National Institutes of Health.

Risky teen driving behaviors decrease when teens and their parents agree on the conditions under which teens can drive. Simply communicating the driving rules to teens is not enough. What reduces risky teen driving is having a common understanding of the rules and the consequences for violating them. Agreement on the context—the where, when, and with whom a teen can drive—reduces risky driving most. Thus agreement about limits on nighttime driving and the number of passengers—conditions known to increase the risk of a car crash—were the most likely to increase safe driving.

Motor vehicle crashes are the leading cause of death and injury among adolescents between the ages of 16 and 20. According to the National Highway Traffic Safety Adminis-

Kenneth H. Beck, Jessica L. Hartos, and Bruce G. Simons-Morton, "Parent-Teen Disagreement of Parent-Imposed Restrictions on Teen Driving After One Month of Licensure: Is Discordance Related to Risky Teen Driving?" *Prevention Science*, vol. 6, September, 2005, pp. 177–185. Copyright © 2005 Springer. Reproduced with kind permission from Springer Science and Business Media and the authors.

tration, in 2001, there were over 1.6 million crashes and over 8700 persons were killed in crashes involving 16–20-year-old drivers. Adolescent crash rates are higher than those of any other age group, and are elevated when teens drive on weekends, with teen passengers, and at nighttime.

A growing body of evidence indicates that parents can play a crucial role in reducing the level of teen driving risk.

The Role of Parents

A growing body of evidence indicates that parents can play a crucial role in reducing the level of teen driving risk. Several investigations have found that teens who report high levels of parental monitoring and driving restrictions are less likely to engage in a variety of risky driving behaviors and to report violations and crashes than are those with fewer restrictions and less monitoring. Further, parents who report frequently supervising their teen's driving and restricting access to a car have teens who report less speeding and more seat belt use.

Overall, the research suggests that parent and teen reports of parental management of teen driving is related to greater teen driver safety. However, teens usually report fewer restrictions than do their parents. . . . Low levels of parent-teen agreement have . . . been detected regarding driving rules (e.g., restrictions on the number and types of passengers allowed in the car when the teen is driving, whether the teen was allowed to drive in bad weather), how often parents taught teens certain driving skills (e.g., how to avoid being an aggressive driver, how to drive safely at night), and whether the teen had actually engaged in a variety of risky driving activities (e.g., being distracted by friends & passengers while driving, going to dangerous places, driving too fast). In addition to teens reporting fewer driving rules and restrictions than their parents, they also report engaging in more risky driving activities such as speeding, going to dangerous places, driving aggressively, etc., than their parents are aware.

Studying Parent-Teen Discordance

Parent and teen disagreements about parenting behaviors are common. Previous research has shown that parent-teen discordance is associated with a variety of high-risk activities, including teen violence, substance use, sexual behavior, and academic achievement. Whereas parent-teen discordance may to some extent be normative, research suggests that parental rules and regulations are more effective when teens perceive that their parents have established expectations for their behaviors and consequences for any violations. This has implications for beginning drivers, as parents are most apt to impose driving restrictions when their teens first become licensed and begin to drive independently. If such restrictions are not perceived to be in effect, parents may be less effective at reducing driving risk during the initial period of licensure when teens are at their greatest risk for crash involvement. . . .

Little is known about relations between parent-teen discordance related to parent-imposed driving restrictions and outcomes related to teen driving behaviors. Recently, a randomized trial was conducted to determine if parents could be encouraged to set and maintain driving restrictions for their newly licensed teens. The intervention consisted of a video which presented the risks of teen driving, introduced the specific name of the program, and featured teens and families who had used and liked the program. It also encouraged families to use a parent-teen driving agreement and offered suggestions as to how restrictions could be strictly adopted initially and then relaxed over time as the teen gains more driving experience and shows more responsible behavior. One week later, parents were sent a newsletter reminder to encourage them to use a driving agreement. The results indicated that parents and their teens who were exposed to this intervention, were more likely to report using a driving agreement for up to 9 months later and to report placing passenger and road restrictions on their teens for up to 4 months, than those in the unexposed control group.

While the effects of this intervention, as well as a similar one, have shown that it is possible to increase parental restrictions on teen driving, especially during the first critical months of independent driving, it is unclear how the degree of parent-teen discordance with these driving restrictions is related to teen driving risk. Thus, the first purpose of this investigation was to determine the levels of parent-teen agreement for a variety of parent restrictions on teen driving. . . .

The second purpose of this investigation was to determine the relationship between discordance on these measures and risky teen driving. . . .

Analyzing the Results

Although parent-teen discordance about parenting behaviors and its relation to negative adolescent outcomes has been well-documented, this is the first study to examine the direct relationship between parent-teen discordance concerning parent-imposed driving restrictions and adolescent risky driving. The results indicated that within the first month of driving, more than 33% of teens said that they drove more than 10 miles/hr [miles per hour] over the speed limit and/or went through a stop sign without stopping completely; 45% switched lanes and weaved through traffic and/or engaged in activities such as eating, talking on a phone, or horsed around or were distracted by passengers; and over 50% said they exceeded the speed limit in residential or school zones. Investigations of somewhat older and more experienced provisionally licensed teens in Maryland also found somewhat comparable rates of risky driving, with over 50–60% reporting that they drove too fast, 35–63% were distracted by friends and passengers, and almost 20–50% reported running through a traffic or stop sign. The frequency of these risky teen driving behaviors seems to increase over time. Thus, there was ample evidence of teen risky driving which allowed us to test our hypothesis that discordance would be related to risky driving behaviors.

A common understanding [between parents and teens] of driving restrictions is more directly related to reduced risky driving.

Findings also indicated that levels of parent-teen agreement ranged considerably across these measures. The greatest degree of discordance was observed for the conditions in which the teen was allowed to drive. Both the mean and range of scores indicated considerable variation in how much agreement there was between parents and teens regarding the conditions in which they are allowed to drive. Considerably less variation and lower levels of disagreement were observed for expectations that teens would follow driving rules or experience consequences (restricted driving privileges), if they did not. Previous reports of the intervention effects have shown that the treatment condition produced a significant reduction in initial teen reports of driving in high risk conditions, including teen passengers and nighttime driving. This investigation showed that the intervention also seemed to produce an increase in the level of parent-teen agreement regarding driving in these high risk conditions (e.g., after dark, in bad weather, etc.). However, the intervention did not focus specifically on talking more frequently with teens about driving rules or the consequences for rule violations. It did attempt to help parents codify what the allowable driving conditions, rules and consequences were. This seems to explain why there were no differences across treatment condition for how frequently rules and consequences were discussed, but there were for the degree of agreement regarding the conditions under which a teen was allowed to drive and the consequences for violating those conditions.

> *Discordance [between parents and teens] about restricted driving conductions was the best predictor of risky teen driving.*

Greater Agreement, Decreased Risk

Greater agreement regarding restricted driving conditions and consequences were significantly associated with decreased teen driving risk. However, agreement regarding talking about driving rules and consequences was not. It may be that parental communication is the means by which driving rules are established, but a common understanding of driving restrictions is more directly related to reduced risky driving. Alternatively, frequency of discussion about rules may increase when parents and teens disagree, rather than agree, about restrictions. It is even possible that in some cases expectations about driving conditions, rules and consequences may have been discussed before the teen obtained his or her license. Thus, for some families it may not have been necessary to discuss these issues again once the teen is driving, or the only time they are discussed is when a rule has been violated. In any event, our findings suggest that the frequency of parental communication about driving rules may be less important to risky teen driving than is a common understanding about what the driving conditions are and the consequences for violating them. It is one thing to have parents say that they impose various rules on their teen's driving; however, if teens do not receive or accept this message then it is unlikely that they will base subsequent behavior on them. Agreement about the frequency of parental communication about the consequences for rule violations was related to concordance of expectations that consequences would occur. This suggests that rules will be taken more seriously if parents have made sure that their teens know and understand that their driving privileges will be restricted for violating them. A driving rule (e.g., call home if you will be late) takes on more meaning if it is understood that failure to do so will result in losing one's driving privileges.

Discordance about restricted driving conditions was the best predictor of risky teen driving. Teens who showed greater agreement (i.e., less discordance) with their parents' reports of the restrictions on the conditions in which they could drive reported fewer risky driving activities in their first month of driving. This suggests that agreement in this situational context (e.g., where, when and with whom a teen can drive) is more important than agreement concerning the established rules for teen driving or the punitive aspects associated with violating restrictions. Subsequent analyses showed that the individual driving conditions with the greatest agreement included restrictions on nighttime driving (a state-imposed legal restriction), driving with teen passengers, and not telling a parent when you will return, where you will be going, or who your passengers will be. Each of these represent the conditions that are most likely to be associated with motor vehicle crash involvement of teens.

Greater parent-teen concordance about parent-imposed driving restrictions is protective against risky teen driving.

Maintaining Restrictions

In addition, lower parent-teen discordance was related to a brief intervention aimed at increasing and maintaining restrictions on teen driving. Parents and teens in the intervention group showed greater agreement related to restricted driving conditions and driving restrictions. However, the intervention was not related to teen risky driving behaviors. The parent intervention may have worked indirectly at reducing risky teen driving by increasing the agreement between teens and their parents concerning the conditions in which teens are allowed to drive, and the consequences for violating rules. Future research should investigate whether a mediated relationship exists between parent-teen discordance and a variety of driver-behavior outcomes.

The findings are consistent with the hypothesis that greater parent-teen concordance about parent-imposed driving restrictions is protective against risky teen driving. Likewise, the greater the discordance between parents and teens, the more teens may be apt to drive in a risky fashion. However, it is unknown the extent to which these findings can be generalized to other samples of teen drivers. Clearly, our sample was derived from a fairly affluent, suburban area of Maryland. Whether risky driving behaviors or concordances with parent-imposed driving restrictions in the first month of licensure would be remarkably different in teens from more rural or less affluent areas are unknown. It is possible that the level of teen risky driving may be higher or lower in less affluent communities than the one studied in this research. In addition, the measures relied upon parent and teen reports of teen driving limits with no outside collaborating source. Of course, self-reported responses are open to social desirability, especially among parents who may report more restrictions than they actually impose because it would be the "right" thing to say.

13

Parents Pass on Bad Driving Habits to Their Teens

Liberty Mutual and Students Against Destructive Decisions

Liberty Mutual is a global insurance group and Students Against Destructive Decisions (SADD) is a peer-to-peer education and prevention organization.

Many teens report that their parents are the biggest influence on their own driving habits. Unfortunately, research reveals that many parents speed and talk on cell phones while driving, behaviors that increase the risk of traffic accidents. In addition, some parents do not wear safety belts, thereby increasing the chance of injury or death in the event of an accident. The fact that many teens do not see these driving practices as unsafe is therefore not surprising. These behaviors are indeed unsafe, and parents must set a better example.

High school and middle school students overwhelmingly say their parents are or will be the biggest influence on how they drive, but the practices many teens say they are emulating represent some of the riskiest driving behaviors, according to the 2004 Liberty Mutual/SADD Teen Driving Study.

"Nearly 60 percent of high school students say their parents are the biggest influence on their driving, and 69 percent of middle school students say parents will be the biggest influence when they do drive," said Liberty Mutual Executive Vice

Liberty Mutual and Students Against Destructive Decisions, "Teens 'Inherit' Parents' Bad Driving Habits," *SADD Teens Today*, August 10, 2004. Copyright © 2000–2007 all rights reserved. Reproduced by permission.

President Paul Condrin. "So when we engage in unsafe driving behaviors, it's no wonder they are inheriting our bad habits behind the wheel."

The Impact of Parent Driving Behaviors

Almost two thirds (62 percent) of high school teens surveyed by Liberty Mutual and SADD (Students Against Destructive Decisions) say their parents talk on a cell phone while driving. Almost half, 48 percent, say their parents speed, and 31 percent say their parents don't wear a safety belt.

Not surprisingly, given the study's finding that many young drivers are influenced by their parents' driving habits, teens say they now follow, or expect to follow, these same practices in roughly the same percentages when they become drivers.

- Sixty-two percent of high school drivers say they talk on a cell phone while driving, and approximately half of high school teens who do not yet drive (52 percent) and middle school students (47 percent) expect they will engage in this behavior when they begin driving.

- Sixty-seven percent of high school drivers say they speed. Interestingly, most high school teens (65 percent) who do not yet drive and middle school students (79 percent) say they would not speed once they got their license.

- Thirty-three percent of high school drivers say they do not wear their safety belt while driving. High school students who do not yet drive (28 percent) and middle school students (20 percent) are less likely to believe they will drive while not wearing a safety belt.

"It is critically important that parents set the example they wish their children to follow. Parents should not be afraid to establish expectations for their young drivers, discuss those expectations frequently, and ensure they are being met," said Stephen Wallace, SADD Chairman and CEO [chief executive officer]. "Five years of Liberty Mutual and SADD research repeatedly shows that teens who have regular communication with their parents about expected behaviors are less likely to make destructive decisions."

A Clear Disconnect

Parental influence on teen drivers may help explain a clear disconnect between how teens view themselves as drivers and their actual driving habits. Nearly nine out of 10 teens (89 percent) describe themselves as safe drivers. Yet many engage in risky behaviors that often lead to crashes, including speeding, neglecting to use safety belts, and talking on a cell phone. What's more, many teens don't view these behaviors as dangerous, again suggesting that they believe they are safe because their parents drive the same way.

- Twenty-seven percent of all high school students and 33 percent of middle school students think speeding is safe.

- Twenty-five percent of all high school students and 29 percent of middle school students say driving without a safety belt is safe.

- Twenty-four percent of high school students and 32 percent of middle school students say talking on a cell phone while driving is safe.

"The inability among teens to appreciate how unsafe their common driving behaviors are is alarming, yet not surprising, given the fact that parents . . . exhibit the same dangerous habits."

"The inability among teens to appreciate how unsafe their common driving behaviors are is alarming, yet not surprising, given the fact that parents and other influencing adults exhibit the same dangerous habits," said Kathryn Swanson, chair of the Governors Highway Safety Association. "The Liberty Mutual/SADD report reminds all parents that we need to be diligent in both telling and showing our children the safest way to drive."

The Risk of Poor Driving Habits

Government and institutional data reveal why it is critically important that projects like the 2004 Liberty Mutual/SADD Teen Driving Study continue to draw attention to poor driving habits in the U.S.

- *Speeding*—According to the Insurance Institute for Highway Safety, speeding is a factor in 31 percent of all fatal crashes, killing an average of 1,000 Americans each month, and the National Highway Traffic Safety Administration (NHTSA) reports speeding is involved in 37 percent of all young driver deaths.

- *Safety Belt Use*—Nearly four in five drivers (79 percent) in the U.S. wore their safety belts in 2003, according to NHTSA, yet safety belt use was only 60 percent in vehicle crashes involving fatalities. NHTSA estimates safety belt use by drivers and occupants saved more than 14,000 lives that year.

- *Cell Phone Use*—While cell phone use as a cause of distracted driving-related accidents is not extensive, NHTSA says drivers in a self-reported study estimated nearly 300,000 crashes from 1998–2002 were the result of cell phone use.

14

Male Teen Passengers Increase Risky Teen Driving

National Institute of Child Health and Human Development

The National Institute of Child Health and Human Development, part of the National Institutes of Health, is the biomedical research arm of the U.S. government and sponsors research on issues that affect children and family health.

Studies show that risky teen driving increases in the presence of male teen passengers. For example, both males and females are more likely to drive faster and more closely to the vehicle in front of them when a male passenger is present. While researchers are not clear why teens engage in riskier behavior with male passengers present, some suggest that male passengers may pose a greater distraction or change the driver's attitudes. Parents and teen drivers should be aware of these risks and restrict the number of passengers a teen driver may carry.

Teenage drivers—both males and females—were more likely to tailgate and exceed the speed limit if there was a teenage male passenger in the front seat, according to a study by the National Institute of Child Health and Human Development [NICHD] of the National Institutes of Health.

Conversely, male teenagers were less likely to tailgate or exceed the speed limit when a teenage female was in the front passenger seat. In addition, female teen drivers were slightly more likely to tailgate if there was a female teen passenger in the vehicle with them. . . .

National Institute of Child Health and Human Development, "Teens' Driving Riskier with Male Teen Passenger; Teen Boys' Driving Safer with Female Teen Passenger," *NIH News*, August 24, 2005.

The Study

"This study provides information that will be useful for officials in devising teen licensing standards," said NICHD Director Duane Alexander, M.D. "The findings indicate that teen risky driving increases in the presence of teen passengers, particularly male teen passengers. But more important, the finding should remind teens—and the adults who care about them—that they need to drive safely, regardless of who is in the passenger seat."

The study was unable to determine why the presence of teen males increased the likelihood of speeding and tailgating, said the study's first author Bruce G. Simons-Morton, Ed.D., M.P.H, Chief of NICHD's Prevention Research Branch.

Crash rates for 16- and 17-year-old drivers are higher in the presence of teen passengers, Dr. Simons-Morton and his colleagues wrote. However, researchers do not understand the reasons for these higher crash rates. Dr. Simons-Morton and colleagues at the survey research firm Westat undertook the current study to learn how the presence of teen passengers might affect teens' driving behavior.

To conduct the study, the researchers positioned observers at the parking lot exits of 10 high schools in the suburban Washington, D.C. area. The observers took notes on the make and model of the departing vehicles, as well as the age and gender of the driver and passengers. A second group of observers was stationed 1/2 to 3/4 of a mile away from the parking lot, and used video recording equipment and a laser-assisted radar device to measure traffic flow. This second set of observers charted the speed of the vehicles and measured vehicle headway, an indication of how closely vehicles follow the vehicles in front of them. The study authors defined vehicle headway as the time (in seconds) between vehicles as they passed a fixed point in the roadway.

More than 3000 passing vehicles were recorded at the second site. Of these, 2251 were vehicles in general traffic, and

471 were teen drivers (245 male and 226 female). No passengers were present in 232 of the teen vehicles, and one or more passengers were present in 239 of the teen vehicles.

The Results

On average, teens drove 1.3 miles an hour [mph] faster than the general traffic. Moreover, the average headway for teen drivers was about .17 seconds shorter than for the general traffic (about 10 feet less at 40 miles an hour).

Both male and female teenage drivers were most likely to drive faster than the general traffic and to allow shorter headways if there was a male teenage passenger in the car. In fact, when a male passenger was in the vehicle, a quarter of teenage drivers exceeded the speed limit by at least 15 miles an hour.

Both male and female teens drove faster and allowed shorter headways in the presence of a male teenage passenger.

Similarly, both male and female teens drove faster and allowed shorter headways in the presence of a male teenage passenger when compared to teens who had either no passengers or a female teen passenger. However, teenage males allowed longer headways in the presence of female passengers.

On average, headways were .3 seconds shorter for male teen drivers with male teen passengers, and .15 seconds shorter for female teen drivers with female teen passengers.

"At typical driving speeds of around 40 mph, a 0.3 [seconds] difference is equivalent to traveling slightly more than one car length closer to the vehicle ahead," the authors wrote.

The Conclusions

In the article, the study authors explained that although they studied vehicle headway and speed independently, these two factors are probably related. "Close following headways may constrain speed; fast driving may result in close following," they wrote.

For this reason, the authors charted the proportion of teens engaging in some form of risky driving, which they defined as either driving with a headway of less than 1 second, and speeds 15 or more miles above the posted speed limit.

According to these criteria, of the 14.9 percent of teen males engaging in risky driving, 21.7 percent had a male teen passenger in the vehicle. In contrast, only 5.5 percent of teen male drivers showed risky driving behavior in the presence of a female passenger.

Of the 13.1 percent of teen female drivers showing risky driving behavior, 12.9 percent had a male teen passenger, and 15.5 percent had a female passenger. Dr. Simons-Morton said that most cases of risky driving in this 15.5 percent of risky teen female drivers were due to short headways.

Dr. Simons-Morton noted that the current study could not identify why teens were more likely to engage in more risky driving behavior in the presence of teen passengers. Teen passengers may distract the driver or change the driver's attitude or emotion in ways that are not yet clear. To find answers, he and his colleagues are currently designing a study that will involve placing electronic monitoring equipment in vehicles with teen drivers. After learning the reasons for the risky behavior, researchers can then work to develop ways to prevent it.

Until answers become available, Dr. Simons-Morton cautioned parents and teens to be aware of a tendency that teens appear to have toward risky driving when other teens are in the vehicle with them, and to be extra vigilant against unsafe driving under these conditions.

15

Passenger Restrictions for Teen Drivers Will Save Lives

Anne T. McCartt

Anne T. McCartt is senior vice president of research at the Insurance Institute for Highway Safety, a research and communications organization funded by auto insurers.

Passengers are a major risk factor for teen drivers, especially if those passengers are themselves teens. The risk of a fatal crash increases considerably when teens drive with teen passengers. For example, speeding and driver error are more frequent in crashes where teen drivers carry teen passengers. Although passenger restrictions may be inconvenient for some parents, the resulting reduction in teen crashes will make such restrictions well worth it.

The young driver problem is well recognized. Less recognized is that the age group most affected by licensing policies—16 year-olds—has by far the highest crash risk among drivers of any age. Nationally the crash risk per miles driven by 16 year-olds is almost twice that for 18–19 year-olds and about 7 times the risk for drivers ages 30–59. The risk pattern is similar for *fatal* crashes involving young drivers.

The Scope of the Problem

The problem is that 16 year-olds are inexperienced drivers. As a group they also are the youngest and most immature licensed drivers. Compared with fatal crashes among older

Anne T. McCartt, "Statement Before the Pennsylvania House Transportation Committee: Passenger Restrictions for Young Drivers," *Insurance Institute for Highway Safety*, July 24, 2007. Copyright © 1996–2006 Insurance Institute for Highway Safety, Highway Loss Data Institute. Reproduced by permission.

drivers, those among teenage drivers, especially 16 year-olds, more often are single-vehicle, run-off-the-road collisions; more often involve speeding; and more often include multiple passengers.

Most teenagers who are fatally injured are drivers, but many teenagers also die as passengers. Nationwide in 2005, 38 percent of motor vehicle occupant deaths among 16–19 year-olds were sustained by passengers, and at age 16 the numbers of driver and passenger deaths essentially were equal. In Pennsylvania 41 percent of motor vehicle deaths among 16–19 year-olds during 1995–2005 were passengers. Among 16 year-olds more than half of occupants killed—54 percent—were passengers.

Nationwide in 2005, more than half of fatally injured teenage passengers ages 14–19 were in vehicles being driven by teenagers. The percentages were highest for 16 and 17 year-olds—70 and 74 percent, respectively.

Young drivers' fatal crashes reveal evidence of increased risk-taking behavior when teenage passengers are present.

Driving with Passengers

A major risk factor for teenage drivers is the presence of passengers, especially teenage passengers. For older drivers, passenger presence either has no effect on crash risk or decreases it; but for young drivers, passengers greatly magnify the risk. That is, teenagers' already high fatal crash risk when driving alone increases dramatically when passengers are added. In a 2000 Institute study, analyses based on passengers of all ages indicated that the driver death rates per million trips for 16 year-olds were 2.0 with no passengers, 2.8 with one passenger, 3.7 with two passengers, and 5.6 with three or more passengers. For 17 year-olds, driver death rates were 1.5 with no passengers, 2.2 with one passenger, 3.8 with two passengers, and 4.5 with three or more passengers.

Characteristics of young drivers' fatal crashes reveal evidence of increased risk-taking behavior when teenage passengers are present. Speeding and driver error are more frequent in crashes with teenage passengers, and these characteristics increase with the number of teenagers in the vehicle.

The reasons why passengers increase crash risk for teenage drivers are obvious. Teenage passengers create distractions for drivers who are inexperienced to start with and who need to be paying full attention to the driving task. Plus the presence of peers in the vehicle may induce young drivers to take risks.

Passenger restrictions can involve some inconveniences for parents. Still, an Institute survey of parents and teenagers shows strong support for graduated licensing in states where it has been adopted and for passenger restrictions where they are in effect.

For example, California's graduated licensing law went into effect in 1998 and was the first to include a meaningful passenger restriction. No passengers younger than 20 were allowed in the vehicle during the first 6 months of licensure unless an adult 25 or older was present. When the Institute surveyed parents, there was strong support for graduated licensing and for the passenger restriction. On January 1, 2006, the law was amended to extend the passenger restriction to the first year of licensure.

National studies of the effects of graduated licensing . . . have reported crash reductions due to passenger restrictions.

The Institute also found that, although graduated licensing limits some teenagers' social activities, four out of five teenagers were able to adapt and participate in these activities anyway. And even though some parents reported occasional inconveniences from the passenger restriction, the majority of the parents surveyed reported no inconveniences.

Thirty-nine states plus the District of Columbia have introduced passenger limitations as part of their graduated licensing systems. Four studies of the initial 6-month passenger restriction in California all indicated positive effects. For example, an Institute study found a 38 percent reduction of 16 year-old drivers in crashes per capita in which teenage passengers were injured or killed. In North Carolina, it has been reported that multiple-passenger crashes declined by 32 percent among 16 year-old drivers, and by 15 percent among 17 year-old drivers, since a passenger restriction was enacted. National studies of the effects of graduated licensing also have reported crash reductions due to passenger restrictions. Given the positive effects of passenger restrictions for young drivers, adopting such a requirement makes sense.

16

Teen Cell Phone Use Restrictions Will Save Lives

Steve Blackistone

Steve Blackistone is a member of the National Transportation Safety Board, an independent federal agency that investigates transportation crashes, determines their probable cause, and makes recommendations to prevent their recurrence.

Adding a cell phone use restriction to state graduated driver licensing programs will reduce death and injury on America's highways. Driver distractions are one of the leading causes of traffic accidents, even more so for teen drivers. For example, one inexperienced teen driver, who was driving at least fifteen miles over the speed limit while talking on a cell phone, lost control of her vehicle. The resulting crash killed five people. States must respond to such tragedies by increasing restrictions on the growing number of teen driver distractions, including the use of cell phones.

The [National Transportation] Safety Board has recognized for many years that traffic crashes are one of this nation's most serious transportation safety problems. More than 90 percent of all transportation related deaths each year result from highway crashes. A disproportionate number of these highway crashes involve teenage drivers between the ages of 15 to 20, young people who have only recently gotten their driver's license.

Steve Blackistone, Testimony Before the Committee on Technology and Energy, Michigan Senate and House Bill 5133—Cell Phone Use Restrictions for Teen Drivers, www.NTSB.org, November 9, 2005.

Addressing the Teen-Driving Problem

In a 1993 review of underage drinking and licensing for young drivers under the age of 21, the Safety Board recommended that States implement graduated driver licensing (GDL), the comprehensive provisional license system for teen drivers. In 2002, the Safety Board revisited this issue and added a passenger restriction to its GDL recommendation. Then, following the investigation of a Maryland crash that killed 5 people in early 2003, the Safety Board recommended that a restriction on cell phone use while driving be added to the graduated licensing system.

In spite of the revolutionary changes in driver licensing practices that have been adopted in recent years, teen drivers continue to be involved in an alarming number of crashes. Traffic crashes are the leading cause of death among teenagers today, accounting for 40 percent of all deaths among 15–20 year olds. Young drivers age 15 through age 20 make up less than 7 percent of the driving population, but compose more than 13.5 percent of the drivers involved in fatal crashes. Further, more than 21 percent of all highway fatalities occur in crashes involving teen drivers. Crash statistics for Michigan are just as ominous. While young drivers are a little more than 7 percent of the driving population, they are more than 14.2 percent of the drivers involved in fatal crashes. More than 22 percent of Michigan's highway fatalities occur in crashes involving teen drivers.

Young drivers have been the focus of U.S. licensing systems primarily because they constitute the largest group of beginners and have the highest crash risk. Studies by the National Highway Traffic Safety Administration (NHTSA), the Insurance Institute for Highway Safety, the States and others have shown that 16-year-olds are more likely to be involved in single vehicle crashes, be responsible for the crash, be cited for speeding, have more passengers than older drivers, and be unbelted. Such fatal crashes are most likely to occur from 10 PM to midnight, primarily on Friday and Saturday nights.

Michigan is to be commended for being one of the first States to adopt a comprehensive graduated licensing system. The current program includes a 3-phase system with a learner's permit, an intermediate license, and a full license. Young drivers must hold their learner's permit for a minimum of 6 months, complete driver education, and obtain at least 50 hours of supervised driving. There is a midnight to 5:00 AM driving restriction during the intermediate phase. However, there is no restriction on cell phone use by young drivers when they are holding a learner's or intermediate license.

The Increase in Drivers Using Cell Phones

We all recognize that cell phone use is becoming increasingly prevalent. The use of these devices has more than tripled, from 60 million subscribers in 1998 to more than 197 million today.

Likewise, increasing numbers of drivers are using cell phones. The National Highway Transportation Safety Administration (NHTSA) has just released research documenting that an estimated 4 percent of drivers were using hand-held cell phones, during daylight hours, in 2002. This translates into approximately 600,000 drivers on the road at any time during the day using hand-held phones. That was a 33 percent increase in 2 years. When combined with data from other surveys about hands-free cell phone use, NHTSA concluded that nearly 900,000 drivers (6 percent) are using a telephone at any given time.

Preliminary results from a survey in 2004 indicate further increases in usage. Driver usage of hand-held cell phones reached 5 percent in 2004, and the use of all phones—both hand-held and hands-free—reached 8 percent. No information is available about text messaging and its use while driving. However, just this week we have been notified of a fatal crash in Hawaii [on November 4, 2005] that involved a lane crossover into oncoming traffic. Local media report that the driver of the vehicle that crossed over into oncoming traffic was text messaging at the time. That is an example of why we recommend using the term "interactive wireless communication device" in lieu of "cell phone" in the law.

The NHTSA survey also found that cell phone use increased among young adults, age 16–24, from 3 percent in 2000 to 5 percent in 2002. That rate is higher than any other age category.

States [should] enact legislation to prohibit holders of learner's permits and intermediate licenses from using interactive wireless communication devices while driving.

The Role of Driver Distraction

In 2003, the Safety Board examined the role that driver distraction plays in motor vehicle crashes, especially when the driver is inexperienced. The Board concluded that current State laws are inadequate to protect young, novice drivers from distractions that can lead to crashes. The Board recommended that States enact legislation to prohibit holders of learner's permits and intermediate licenses from using interactive wireless communication devices while driving.

The recommendation is derived from the Board's investigation of a Ford Explorer Sport collision with a Ford Windstar minivan and a Jeep Grand Cherokee on Interstate 95/495 near Largo, Maryland. On February 1, 2002, at about 8:00 PM, a Ford Explorer Sport was traveling northbound on the outer loop of the Capitol Beltway (Interstate 95/495) near Largo, Maryland at an estimated speed of 70 to 75 mph [miles per hour], when it veered off the left side of the roadway, crossed over the median, climbed up a guardrail, flipped over and landed on top of a southbound Ford Windstar minivan.

Subsequently, a 1998 four-door Jeep Grand Cherokee ran into the rear of the minivan. Of the eight people involved in the accident, five adults were killed, one adult sustained minor injuries, and two children were uninjured.

[One teen driver involved in a fatal crash] was driving 15–20 miles over the speed limit, while talking on a hand-held wireless telephone.

This crash involved multiple risk factors, some of which are associated with young drivers. The unbelted crash driver, who had only an estimated 50 hours of driving experience, was operating a short-wheelbase sport utility vehicle, with which she was unfamiliar. She was driving 15–20 miles over the speed limit, while talking on a hand-held wireless telephone.

Learning how to drive and becoming comfortable in traffic requires all the concentration a novice driver can muster. A 2001 study found that even experienced drivers engaged in wireless telephone conversations were unaware of traffic movements around them.

Restricting Cell Phone Use While Driving

In January 2002, New Jersey became the first State to restrict phone use by young novice drivers. Its new law prohibited holders of special learner's permits, driver's examination permits, and provisional driver's licenses from using any interactive wireless communication device while operating a motor vehicle. Today there are 10 States that restrict cell phone use by drivers with an instructional and/or intermediate license. The Safety Board recommends that you prohibit the use of any wireless communication device, hand-held or hands-free, by holders of learner's permits or provisional licenses, under age 18.

Let me also briefly mention one other important improvement to Michigan's graduated licensing system that is now pending before the Senate. That is the addition of a restriction on the number of passengers that drivers in the graduated licensing system may carry. Teen drivers drive with more passengers than older drivers, and these passengers are usually the drivers' peers. These passengers create a deadly combination of distraction, inexperience and immaturity. The relative risk of death among 16- and 17-year-old drivers increases when there is a single passenger, and that risk grows each time the number of passengers grows. Carrying at least three teen passengers results in a threefold increase in the probability of a teen in that vehicle suffering a fatal injury.

Based on the available research and accident data, the Safety Board concluded that by restricting to zero or one the number of passengers carried by young novice drivers during the provisional (intermediate) license stage, States can reduce crashes involving young novice drivers and reduce fatalities among teenage occupants. The Board, therefore, believes that Michigan should restrict young novice drivers with a graduated license from carrying more than one passenger under the age of 20 until they receive an unrestricted license or for at least 6 months (whichever is longer). Currently, 20 States and the District of Columbia, including your neighbors of Indiana, Illinois, and Wisconsin, have enacted passenger restrictions.

A cell phone use restriction . . . will save both young lives and the lives of others involved in crashes with young drivers.

Highway crashes involving young drivers will remain a serious and persistent problem unless concrete and comprehensive steps are taken. Our young people are this nation's most valuable resource, and should be nurtured and protected. Too many of them are being killed and injured unnecessarily.

The Safety Board is so convinced of the life saving benefit of graduated licensing with a cell phone restriction that it recently was added to our list of "Most Wanted" safety recommendations. Adding a cell phone use restriction, such as provided in H.B. [House bill] 5133, will significantly strengthen the graduated licensing system in Michigan. It will save both young lives and the lives of others involved in crashes with young drivers.

Organizations to Contact

The editors have compiled the following list of organizations concerned with the issues debated in this book. The descriptions are derived from materials provided by the organizations. All have publications or information available for interested readers. The list was compiled on the date of publication of the present volume; the information provided here may change. Be aware that many organizations take several weeks or longer to respond to inquiries, so allow as much time as possible.

Advocates for Highway and Auto Safety
750 First St. NE, Ste. 901, Washington, DC 20002
(202) 408-1711 • fax: (202) 408-1699
e-mail: advocates@saferoads.org
Web site: www.saferoads.org

Advocates for Highway and Auto Safety is an alliance of consumer, health and safety groups, and insurance companies that seek to make America's roads safer. The alliance advocates the adoption of federal and state laws, policies, and programs that save lives and reduce injuries. On its Web site, the organization publishes fact sheets, press releases, polls, and reports as well as links to legislative reports and testimony on federal legislation involving traffic safety, including issues surrounding teen driving.

American Driver & Traffic Safety Education Association (ADTSEA)
Highway Safety Center, Indiana University of Pennsylvania
R & P Bldg., Indiana, PA 15705
(724) 357-3975 • fax: (724) 357-7595
e-mail: support@hsc.iup.edu
Web site: http://adtsea.iup.edu

ADTSEA works with driver's education instructors and state authorities to improve driver's education standards and practices. On its Web site, ADTSEA publishes white papers, articles, and reports, including *Brain Development and Risk-Taking in Adolescent Drivers, Suggested Standards for the Improvement of Driver Education,* and *Parent-Teen Driving Agreements: Contracts for Safety?*

Century Council

1310 G Street NW, Ste. 600, Washington, DC   20005
(202) 637-0077 • fax: (202) 637-0079
e-mail: millsl@centurycouncil.org
Web site: www.centurycouncil.org

Funded by America's leading distillers, the Century Council is a not-for-profit, national organization committed to fighting underage drinking and reducing alcohol-related traffic crashes. The council promotes legislative efforts to pass tough drunk driving laws and works with the alcohol industry to help servers and sellers prevent drunk driving. Its interactive virtual campus, Alcohol 101 Plus, provides "virtual" scenarios to help students make sensible, fact-based decisions about drinking. The site can be found at www.alcohol101plus.org.

Highway Safety Research Center
(at the University of North Carolina)

730 Martin Luther King Jr. Blvd., CB #3430
Chapel Hill, NC   27599
(919) 962-2202 • fax: (919) 962-8710
Web site: www.hsrc.unc.edu

The goal of the University of North Carolina Highway Safety Research Center is to improve the safety, security, access, and efficiency of all surface transportation modes through research, evaluation, and information dissemination. It publishes the quarterly newsletter, *Directions,* recent issues of which are available on its Web site. The center's online "Research Library" link provides access to fact sheets, articles, and reports on traffic safety issues such as teen driving, including *Improving Graduated Driver Licensing Systems: A Conceptual Approach and Its Implications* and *Parental Supervision of Teenage Drivers in a Graduated Licensing System.*

Insurance Institute for Highway Safety (IIHS)

1005 N. Glebe Rd., Ste. 800, Arlington, VA   22201
(703) 247-1500 • fax: (703) 247-1588
Web site: www.hwysafety.org

IIHS is a nonprofit research and public information organization funded by auto insurers. The institute conducts research to find effective measures to prevent motor vehicle crashes, including those that result from teen driving. On its Web site, the institute publishes information on the results of its research by topic. The "Teenagers" link includes fatality statistics, articles on teen driving from the institute's newsletter, Status Report, tables of each state's teen driving laws, and institute congressional testimony on issues related to teen driving.

National Highway Traffic Safety Administration (NHTSA)

1200 New Jersey Ave. SE, West Building
Washington, DC   20590
(888) 327-4236
Web site: www.nhtsa.dot.gov

The function of NHTSA is to save lives, prevent injuries, and reduce economic costs due to road traffic crashes through education, research, safety standards, and enforcement activity. Its Driving Licensing Division supports states' efforts to enact improved graduated driver licensing laws. It also develops standards for driver education instructors and a standardized driver education curriculum. Its Teen Drivers "Quick Click" link provides access to fact sheets, articles, and reports on teen driving issues.

National Organizations for Youth Safety (NOYS)

7371 Atlas Walk Way, Ste. 109, Gainesville, VA   20155
(703) 981-0264 • fax: (703) 754-8262
e-mail: sspavone@noys.org
Web site: www.noys.org

NOYS is a collaborative network of national organizations and federal agencies that serve youth and focus on youth safety and health, particularly traffic safety. On its Web site, NOYS provides access to research and resources on teen driving, including "Preventing Teen Motor Crashes."

National Safety Council
1121 Spring Lake Dr., Itasca, IL   60143
(630) 285-1121 • (630) 285-1315 fax
e-mail: info@nsc.org
Web site: www.nsc.org

Founded in 1913 and chartered by the U.S. Congress in 1953, the NSC is a nonprofit, nongovernmental, public service organization dedicated to protecting life and promoting health. Members include businesses, labor organizations, schools, public agencies, private groups, and individuals. The council conducts research and provides information on highway safety. The NSC publishes the yearly *Injury Facts* and the *Journal of Safety Research*. On its Web site, NSC publishes fact sheets on key safety issues, including "Teen Driving."

Students Against Destructive Decisions (SADD)
PO Box 800, Marlboro, MA   01752
(877) SADD-INC • fax: (508) 481-5759
e-mail: info@sadd.org
Web site www.saddonline.com

Formerly called Students Against Drunk Driving, SADD is a school-based organization dedicated to addressing the issues of underage drinking, impaired driving, drug use, and other destructive decisions that harm young people, including destructive teen driving decisions. SADD seeks to provide students with prevention and intervention tools that build the confidence needed to make healthy choices and behavioral changes. SADD publishes a semiannual newsletter, *Decisions*, recent issues of which are available on its Web site. Also on its Web site, SADD provides access to editorials and articles in its online magazine, *Teens Today*, and fact sheets on teen driving within its "Issues/Driving" link.

Traffic Injury Research Foundation (TIRF)
171 Nepean St., Ste. 200, Ottawa, Ontario K2P 0B4 CA
(613) 238-5235 • fax: (613) 238-5292
e-mail: deanm@trafficinjuryresearch.com
Web site: www.trafficinjuryresearch.com

Founded in 1964, TIRF is an independent road safety institute that seeks to reduce traffic-related deaths and injuries by designing, promoting, and implementing effective programs and policies based on sound research. TIRF publications include brochures, the *TIRF Bulletin* and technical reports, including *Reducing the Crash Risk for Young Drivers* and *Best Practices for Graduated Driver Licensing in Canada*, which are available on its Web site.

Bibliography

Books

Donna R. Crossman and Richard Crossman	*Sixteen Is Too Young to Drive: Taking Control When Your Teen's Behind-the-Wheel*. Scotia, NY: Footnote, 2002.
Karen Gravelle	*The Driving Book: Everything New Drivers Need to Know but Don't Know to Ask*. New York: Walker Books for Young Readers, 2005.
Jim Hinkley and Jon G. Robertson	*The Big Book of Car Culture: The Armchair Guide to Automotive Americana*. Osceola, WI: Motorbooks International, 2005.
Leon James	*Road Rage and Aggressive Driving: Steering Clear of Highway Warfare*. Amherst, NY: Prometheus, 2000.
National Safety Council	*Teen Driver: A Family Guide to Teen Driver Safety*. Itasca, IL: National Safety Council, 2004.
Jon Savage	*Teenage: The Creation of Youth Culture*. New York: Viking, 2007.
Timothy C. Smith	*Crashproof Your Kids: Make Your Teen a Safer, Smarter Driver*. New York: Simon & Schuster, 2006.

Traci Truly

Teen Rights (and Responsibilities): A Legal Guide for Teens and the Adults in Their Lives. Naperville, IL: Sphinx, 2005.

Adam Winters

Everything You Need to Know About Being a Teen Driver. New York: Rosen, 2000.

Periodicals

Joni Balter

"Thumbs Down to Text Messaging," *Seattle Times*, May 10, 2007.

Sherry Boschert

"Gradual Privileges Put Teens Safely in Driver's Seat," *Family Practice News*, October 15, 2005.

Gary Boulard

"Driving Under Experienced," *State Legislatures*, June 2006.

Jodi Cohen

"Driver's Ed Costs in High Gear," *Chicago Tribune*, January 8, 2004.

Thomas S. Dee, David C. Grabowski, and Michael A. Morrisey

"Graduated Driver Licensing and Teen Traffic Fatalities," *Journal of Health Economics*, 2005.

Robert D. Foss

"Improving Graduated Driver Licensing Systems: A Conceptual Approach and Its Implications," *Journal of Safety Research*, February 2007.

Samantha Ganey

"For Teen Drivers, Mom's Monitoring," *Washington Post*, June 1, 2004.

James Hedlund et al.   "What We Know, What We Don't Know, and What We Need to Know About Graduated Licensing," *Journal of Safety Research*, January 2003.

John Holevoet   "Rules Don't Enhance Safety," *USA Today*, March 1, 2005.

Frederick Kunkle and Elizabeth Williamson   "Safety Experts Doubt Benefits of Driver's Ed: Lots of Practice with Parent Seen as Surest Way to Learn," *Washington Post*, November 22, 2004.

Kate Lombardi   "Mom, May I Have the Keys?" *New York Times*, September 28, 2003.

Sarah Mahoney   "What Was He Thinking? Don't Blame It All on Hormones," *Prevention*, March 1, 2004.

Jayne O'Donnell   "Deadly Teen Auto Crashes Show a Pattern," *USA Today*, February 28, 2005.

Stephen L. Oesch   "Passenger Restrictions for Young Drivers," Insurance Institute for Highway Safety, February 9, 2005.

Jordon Rau   "Teen Drivers Could Face Ban on Use of Cell Phones," *Los Angeles Times*, April 25, 2004.

Kathleen Schalch   "Graduated Licensing Cuts Teen-Driving Dangers," *NPR: All Things Considered*, October 10, 2006.

Jeffery Silva   "Mixed Messages and Teen Driving Don't Mix," *RCR Wireless News*, September 26, 2005.

Nick Timiraos   "Teen Driving Curbs Show Results,"
Stateline.org, August 9, 2005.

Shankar
Vedantam   "Teen Passengers a Driving Risk,"
Washington Post, August 29, 2005.

David Weinstein   "It Takes a Village," *(New Jersey)
Times*, July 17, 2007.

Patrick Welsh   "Sweet 16, Not for Driving," *USA
Today*, November 29, 2004.

Index

A

Airbags, 29–30
Alcohol, marijuana, medications, 28–29, 82
American Automobile Association (AAA), 35, 40, 42
American Driver and Traffic Safety Education Association (ADTSEA), 16, 18
Attention-deficit/hyperactivity disorder (ADHD), 31

B

Biological factors, 22
Blood alcohol concentration (BAC), 7, 28, 34
BMW, 68
Brain development, 26, 43, 49, 76–77, 80–81

C

California, 47–48, 53
California Office of Traffic Safety, 14
Cato Institute, 10, 17
Cellular phones, 54, 97, 108–110, 112
Center for Applied Research, 16
Centers for Disease Control (CDC), 12
Cochrane Review Group, 68
Community partnerships, 41
Crashes, 38, 52

D

DaimlerChrysler Corporation, 12
DeKalb study, 16, 65

Driver distractions, 30, 54, 108–109
Driver education
    agenda definition, 74
    appeal, 68
    course duration, 64
    effectiveness, 14–16, 63
    evaluating, 63–64
    international, 65–67, 69
    public support for, 63–64, 69
    research, 71–72
    results, 66
    standards, 16–18
    state-approved programs, 73
Driver's Education Renaissance (IIHS article), 71
Driving
    age, 21–23, 77–79
    conditions, 46–47
    experience, 25–26, 44–47, 59–60, 80

E

Enforcement, 9, 19, 62

F

Fatal accidents, statistics, 24–25, 32–39, 78–79
Fatality Analysis Reporting System (FARS), 7, 35
    methods, definitions, 36–38
Fatigue, 19
Federal Highway Administration, 85
Ford Motor Company, 68
Foundation for Traffic Safety, 42
Freedom, responsibility, 52

G

Governors Highway Safety Association (GHSA), 17, 23, 97
Graduated driver's licenses (GDLs)
AAA and, 40–41
adjustments, 61
California, 47–48, 53
compliance, 61–62
history, 8–9
impact, 13–14, 18–19, 57–58
Michigan, 108, 110–111

H

Harsha, Barbara, 17

I

Insurance Institute for Highway Safety (IIHS), 8, 12, 53–54, 70, 80, 84

J

Journal of Safety Research, 13, 19, 53

L

Liberty Mutual/SADD Driving Study, 94–97
Liberty Mutual Insurance, 14
Licensure delay, 59–61

M

Male teenagers, 98–101
Media reporting, 50, 62, 109
Michigan, 108, 110–111
Minimum driving age, 21–23
Mothers Against Drunk Driving (MADD), 7

N

National Center for Health Statistics, 19
National Center for Statistics and Analysis, 29
National Highway Transportation Safety Administration (NHTSA), 12, 35, 52, 68, 86, 107–108
National Institute of Child Health and Human Development (NICHD), 98–99
National Institute of Health (NIH), 76
National Institute of Mental Health (NIMH), 43
National Minimum Drinking Age Act (NMDAA), 7
National Motorists Association (NMA), 10, 15
National Safety Council, 52, 55
National Transportation Safety Board (NTSB), 17, 68, 106–107
Nighttime driving, 19–20, 27–28, 53–55, 77
Nonmotorists, 37
Nonpassenger vehicles, 37

O

Oregon Department of Transportation (ODOT), 16
Organization for Economic Cooperation and Development, 62

P

Parents, 23
driving behaviors, 95
influence, 94–96
intervention, 87–90, 92
involvement, 41

parent-teen discordance,
88–93
supervision, 62, 78
Passenger vehicles, 36
Politics, 49

R

*Real World Driver: Driving Skills
for Life* program, 68
Recreational driving, 20
Risk-taking, 22, 26, 29, 44, 89–93,
98–101

S

SADD (Students Against Destructive Decisions), 9, 14, 17, 54
Safe Performance Curriculum
group, 65
Safety belts, 29–30, 61, 94–97
Socioeconomic status, 43–47
Speeding, 97–101
Students Against Destructive Decisions (SADD), 9, 14, 17, 54

T

Teen Crashes: Everyone Is at Risk
(AAA study), 42
Teen driving
adult *vs.*, 45–46, 49–50
limits, 18–19
statistics, 24–25, 33–34, 38–39
teenage passengers, 20–21,
26–27, 34, 54–55, 102–105,
111

U

U.S. Census Bureau, 85
U.S. Department of Transportation, 7
Unlicensed drivers, 31
Unsafe cars, 30
USA Today (newspaper), 83–84

W

Wallace, Stephen, 17

Y

Youth Risk Behavior Surveillance
Study, 28